# Philoso
# Part I: Knowledge

# Book Series
## *Philosophy for Heroes*

**Part I: Knowledge**

# PHILOSOPHY FOR HEROES
## PART I: KNOWLEDGE

Published by Clemens Lode Verlag e.K., Düsseldorf

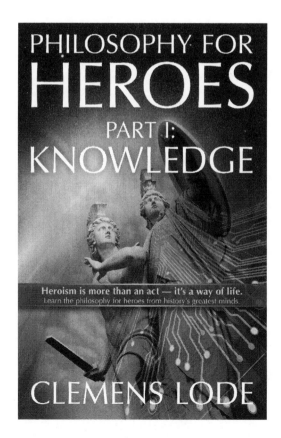

*Clemens Lode Verlag e.K.*, Düsseldorf
https://www.lode.de

2016, First Edition

ISBN 978-3-945586-21-1

Edited by: *Conna Craig*
Book cover design: *Jessica Keatting Graphic Design*
Image sources: *shutterstock, istockphoto*
Icons made by http://www.freepik.com from
http:www.flaticon.com is licensed by CC 3.0 BY
(http://creativecommons.org/licenses/by/3.0/)

Printed on acid-free, unbleached paper.

Subscribe to our newsletter. Simply write to newsletter@lode.de or
visit our website.

PHILOSOPHY
POPULAR SCIENCE
PSYCHOLOGY

# Dedication

 We are, each of us, privileged to live a life that has been touched by many heroes. They possessed extraordinary gifts, and they shared them with us freely. None of these gifts were more remarkable than their ability to discern what needed to be done, and their unfailing courage in doing it and speaking the truth, whatever the personal cost. Let us each strive to accept their gifts and pass them along, as an ongoing tribute to the wise men and women of our human history who taught us all how to be heroes. Do not let the hero in your soul perish in lonely frustration for the life you deserve, but have never been able to reach. Check your road and the nature of your battle. The world you desire can be won, it exists, it is real, it is possible, it is yours.

— Inspired by *Justice League, Hereafter* (DC Comics) and *Atlas Shrugged* (Ayn Rand)

## Introduction

神の一手—*Kami no Itte*—Japanese, roughly meaning "move of God" or "godly move"—describes a completely new insight concerning a move during the game called "Go." Such a move is a goal taught to students to be more attentive toward less obvious maneuvers, leading the students to focus on alternatives. Likewise in philosophy, first put the conspicuous answers aside, to make way for an objective mind and attention to alternatives. Philosophy is much more than a train of thought we contemplate, and does not exclusively serve to stimulate the brain. Philosophy is the foundation of every human being who wants to function in this world, who strives for the *best life possible*, reaching for the greatest potential. Philosophy is part of us and permeates every decision we make.

T<small>HIS BOOK SHOWS</small> some of the 神の一手—*Kami no Itte*—of philosophy and the sciences and combines them into a new view of our inner and outer worlds. The book series *Philosophy for Heroes* offers the intellectual and moral know-how necessary to withstand a chaotic world in a responsible manner, and to become a shining example for others.

# Contents

## The Book Series *Philosophy for Heroes*      173

## The Creation of this Book Series      177

## The Author      187

## Reflection      191

## Kami no Itte      193

## Glossary      197

## Quotation Sources      203

## Bibliography      205

# Publisher's Note

 At LODE Publishing, our commitment is to build a better world through the cultivation of principled leaders. LODE Publishing was founded to curate and publish the highest quality books on philosophy, science, and psychology. *Philosophy for Heroes* is the publisher's inaugural series.

—LODE Publishing, *Mission Statement*

Here are so many facets of launching a publishing company —from concept to design, research, marketing, quality assurance, handling the legal and international aspects of publications—that it is not easy to describe what I do. If I had to narrow it down to one word, though, it might surprise you: dreamer. My dream is a better world, one in which a philosophy of the leader as a hero is embraced and celebrated. This dream is the foundation of LODE Publishing.

As we launch this enterprise, my dream of a better world, and how LODE Publishing will contribute to that world, is the ultimate standard upon which the company's business decisions are based. I look beyond mundane obstacles to paint a picture of how the company might be in five, 10, or even 20 years. The idea of creating a company around a dream allows the company to inject energy into researching, studying, and promoting what it means to equate leadership with heroism. As we move ahead, I look forward to sharing with you the milestones that we reach.

The book has been painstakingly edited by my editor and me. She and I are interested in your comments, thoughts, additions, and in any positive examples of you using the guidelines in this book. To send general feedback, mention the book title in the subject of your message and simply send it to feedback@lode.de. You can also contact us at https://www.lode.de/contact at any time if you are having a problem with any aspect of the book, and we will do our best to address it. Also, I cordially invite you to join our network at https://www.lode.de.

Although we have taken every care to ensure the accuracy of our content, mistakes do happen. If you find a mistake in one of our books, we would be grateful if you would report this to us. By doing so, you can help us to improve subsequent versions of this book and maybe save future readers from frustration. If you find any errata, please report them by visiting https://www.lode.de/errata, selecting your book, and entering the details. Once your errata are verified, your submission will be accepted and the errata will be uploaded to our website, or added to any list of existing errata, under the Errata section of that title. You will, of course, be credited if you wish.

And now that you know what this is about, I thank *you, the reader*, for keeping up the tradition of reading books and supporting the project by your interest in this topic. You and your fellow readers have created a market for this book. I hope that we can fulfill your expectations and we are looking forward to feedback from your side, no matter whether it is positive or negative. This is the only way the project can grow.

- What did you genuinely like about the book?
- What can we improve?
- What subjects would you like to read more about?
- Tell your story! How did you find the book?

Do you have a different view? Let us know what you thought about the book—whether you liked it or not—via contact@lode.de or directly via our network https://www.lode.de/contact. This will help us to develop future titles.

**Best regards,**

**Clemens Lode**
**CEO, Clemens Lode Verlag e.K.**
**Düsseldorf, Germany, November 1st, 2016**

# Preface

 The unicorn lived in a lilac wood, and she lived all alone. She was very old, though she did not know it, and she was no longer the careless color of sea foam but rather the color of snow falling on a moonlit night. But her eyes were still clear and unwearied, and she still moved like a shadow on the sea.

—Peter S. Beagle, *The Last Unicorn*

 THE DECISION to write this book series was born out of an idea: put on paper, in an orderly fashion, the results of my investigations into a number of central questions of life. I see the process of researching, writing, and editing the text as deeply spiritual, with a lot of self-reflection on the one side, and an "inner cleansing" on the other. It helps me to bring about a kind of intellectual closure and allows me to move on to other subjects. This book series has a future to which I am about to embark by writing the next part. But it also has a past. If you want to know the story of this book, please review "The Creation of this Book Series" at the end of the book.

We are each heroes in the making. How can this be? *Because we can reflect on our actions.* We have the potential to become heroes in every aspect and every action of our lives.

Being a hero is much more than committing a heroic act. One does not magically morph into a "hero" as a result of circumstance: the just-in-time rescue, rising up in the midst of a crisis, or even leading others out of a catastrophe. Becoming a hero is more than even these courageous acts. It requires deep insight—the type of philosophical investigation that the greatest minds throughout history have pondered.

In *Philosophy for Heroes: Knowledge*, the first book in a four-book series, we examine the concept of heroism and the foundations of knowledge:

- What is the basis of our understanding of the world?

- How does society define a "hero"?

- How do basic skills, such as language and mathematics, train our way of thinking and reasoning?

Becoming a hero requires more than courage. It requires speaking up, stepping forward from the sidelines, and taking action. For all of this, a deep insight into philosophy is the first, and most important, step. My goal with *Philosophy for Heroes* is to connect the wisdom of the ages to today's real world. If becoming a hero is what you want, *Philosophy for Heroes* is for you.

The topics discussed here are extensive. The entire book series is best understood when viewed as a system of interwoven ideas, some of which can be grasped only with an understanding of all their related elements. Thus, I ask you for patience—if some expression or statement meets your disapproval, consider it within the complete scope of ideas. If we were to show many of today's dominating worldviews on a canvas, some of the topics discussed would likely appear to be out of line. The purpose of *Philosophy for Heroes*, however, is not to repair prevailing worldviews, but to start afresh on a completely new canvas, and comprehend the world from a different perspective.

I will attempt to present this new perspective by building bridges to other philosophies and to science. While I have cited works of others frequently, this book series will present my own point of view. Especially with remarks I have made without references, these are my own ruminations and may be taken merely as starting points for the reader to think about further. The compact nature of *Philosophy for Heroes*, as it touches on a great number of topics, requires this methodology.

Another challenge is deciding which premises to share with you, the reader, first. We have not yet agreed upon a common language, so I will do my best to define and explain the basic concepts as succinctly and clearly as possible. That is the reason I will explain, from the ground up, many terms and situations which (supposedly) are already familiar. It is important to put on the table even those issues that seem obvious and to examine them closely.

Get yourself something to drink, have a seat in a beautiful place, and make yourself comfortable. You have the power to decide freely for yourself. You have the ability to change your life and the world!

Ask yourself a few questions: "Why am I alive? How do I picture myself? What would I like to be?" If your future self could look back at you now, which outstanding qualities and characteristics would he or she recognize? In your core, what is *your* passion in life? What condition or which goals do you strive to reach?

You need not know the answers to those questions yet. While our environment and our values can change from year to year, deep inside, each of us has a unique identity with which we feel comfortable and want to experience. If we recognize our strengths and work on our weaknesses, we might not be able to achieve our goals immediately, but we can wake up every day with the wonderful feeling of having gotten a little closer to our ideal. The ideal is a world in which we reside in harmony with ourselves and our environment, whether in the form of a hectic or calm surroundings, whether socially engaged or not, whether successful in our profession or at peace at home, whether with recognition or inner calm. You can discover your own ideal, but you cannot force others to make that ideal a reality. One of the best ways to get there is to lead by example.

My hope is that you will take with you one or two interesting thoughts from this book series, and develop them further or let them inspire you. Personally, I would like to place this book in the hands of a younger version of myself, someone who finds himself at the beginning of his journey, ready to explore the world. Even if I reach only a small handful of people who will take to heart a few of these core ideas and set out to achieve something great in life themselves —whatever that might be—I will be able to enjoy the rewards of this book. I made the book available to the general public just as I would plant a handful of seeds in the earth, hoping that they grow and bloom.

You, the reader, are holding the open book in your hands and now have an idea of what to expect. Let us now start our journey to become such a shining example for others, thus getting closer to our ideal world.

The path to our goal is the *Philosophy for Heroes.*

**Clemens Lode**
**Author, *Philosophy for Heroes: Knowledge***
**Düsseldorf, Germany, November 1st, 2016**

# Chapter 1

---

# My Philosophy

 No one should postpone the study of philosophy when he is young, nor should he weary of it when he becomes mature, because the search for mental health is never untimely or out of season. To say that the time to study philosophy has not yet arrived or that it has passed is like saying that the time for happiness is not yet at hand or is no longer present.

—Epicurus, *The Art of Happiness*

## 1.1 Heroism

My JOURNEY INTO philosophy started with this quote:

> My philosophy, in essence, is the concept of man as a heroic being, with his own happiness as the moral purpose of his life, with productive achievement as his noblest activity, and reason as his only absolute.

—Ayn Rand, *Atlas Shrugged*

---

### Biography—**Ayn Rand**

Ayn Rand was born in 1905 in the Russian Empire and studied history and philosophy. Inspired by the movies and pictures and disgusted by the communist Soviet Union, she decided to emigrate to the United States: only there could she write freely. She became famous for her two novels, *The Fountainhead* (1943) and *Atlas Shrugged* (1957). She defended *reason* as the only means to acquire knowledge about the world, she was a proponent of rational egoism, and she thought of the initiation of force—be it in the form of a state (dictatorship) or the lack thereof (anarchy)—to reach one's goals as immoral. Ultimately, she propagated *laissez-faire* capitalism with individual rights at its base as the ideal. Her tireless work for individualism and a world of heroes is what makes her a heroine as well.

The term "hero" is problematic because it is used with the very best as well as with the very worst intentions. To call someone a hero is to give him tremendous power and raise him to a position where he must not be questioned. For example, dictatorships usually seize upon this powerful concept and elevate a person to a god-like status. People can speak out against laws and regulations, but who wants to speak out against the person he or she is expected to adore and worship: the hero of the people? For these reasons, we have to examine closely what a "hero" really is.

### 1.1.1 The Conventional Hero

 Men have to have heroes, but no man can ever be as big as the need, and so a legend grows around a grain of truth, like a pearl.

—Peter S. Beagle, *The Last Unicorn*

Conventional heroes often appear in times of crisis or in individual critical situations. Mostly by coincidence, they happen to be on the scene when a person of exceptional strength is required. Their heroic acts are then measured according to the evil or challenge facing them and according to their sacrifice. But the heroic act does not change the person doing it, and the accolade of the public ends eventually. After the situation has been resolved, the hero usually returns back to ordinary life—disenchanted, since he cannot survive daily life through self-sacrifice alone. It is as if those writers with a conventional concept of a hero know that their heroes could not keep up with the idealistic image that people project on them. They do not grow beyond their own sacrifice, leading to many stories ending with the heroic act or the death of the hero.

> **Did you know?**
>
> In the book series *Lord of the Rings* by J. R. R. Tolkien, the hero Bilbo undergoes a long journey to destroy evil once and for all. Through magical explanations, it is assumed that evil will not return once a magic ring is destroyed. In the story, after the heroic deed is done, the "resolution" for the hero is to sail away to another country and spend the rest of his life there. This idea of a final resolution of a problem is the traditional way of portraying a hero. But in reality, the real task would be only beginning: One would have to ask, how did the people turn evil in the first place? How can we educate them to prevent a similar disaster in the future?
>
> $\longrightarrow$ Read more in *Philosophy for Heroes: Epos*

A hero is not *created* by a catastrophe. While an outstanding action *can* point to an actually outstanding character, just because a person happens to help put out a fire or save a child, this itself does *not* necessarily constitute true heroism, even though the deed is of course rewarded with gratitude and recognition. Such a "hero" born of coincidence will be forgotten as fast as he has risen. The elevation of a person to the status of "hero" is only an expression of appreciation for his heroic deed, not for his character traits. There are too many people celebrated as "heroes" who are then falsely viewed as *moral* authorities. Heroic acts are consequences—not causes—of such an authority. Rather than discussing how to imitate heroic acts, or for which causes someone should sacrifice himself, the essence of this book series is how to achieve true moral authority to fulfill the role of a hero, with or without performing "heroic acts." Such acts with public appeal might follow from being able to make the right decisions at the right time. But those acts and the accolades should not be the sole motivation to be moral. We should work toward a world that does not require the sacrifice of individuals.

That is in stark contrast to most movies where experts and organizations of a society are portrayed as being incompetent, and only an extraordinary hero can rescue the world. As "heroes," it is important to know our limits and focus on our strengths instead of trying to carry the whole world on our own shoulders. We do not have to feel responsible for everything that is happening, only to then complain that we cannot manage it on our own. There are experts who can help in their field a lot more effectively than we can. If the actual result is more important to us than the recognition, we have a simpler option to improve the world without having to sacrifice ourselves— we can donate to causes that advance the well-being of others.

**Question**

What are false heroes, and how does a true hero interact with them?

Many seek social recognition for the work they do, for their effort, and ultimately for decisions to sacrifice short-term gratification for long-term goals. For this reason, the title "hero" is the highest honor, reflecting a moral authority others can look up to and emulate to improve their own lives. Using social recognition as our *primary* motivation for heroism fails because it requires us to depend on the moral authority of society, which (at least in times of crisis) is exactly what we want to break with our heroic acts. Thus, apart from natural disasters, a hero aligns him or herself with *reason*, regardless of whether it is with or against trends and public opinion. A true hero stands up to false heroes.

**Idea**

A true hero stands up to false heroes.

Heroism is not simply self-sacrifice. Heroism is possessing the foresight to take a stand for your own values. Heroism is not limited to overcoming a present conflict; it requires fully and consistently taking a stand for a cause and living your life accordingly. While obstacles are part of daily life, and while we can use them to grow, true heroes do not need *emergency* situations; they are not reactive but instead *prepared*, *foresighted*, and intimidating to their adversaries.

They can, however, also be intimidating to their *admirers*. For that reason, we must remember that a hero's acts are *contextual*. A simple smile can be a heroic act in the right situation.

> Even if we do not worship our heroes, they may cow us. It takes a certain amount of confidence and courage to say, "I can do something. I can change this and make a difference." But if you, as a writer think, "What are my words next to those of my hero, Shakespeare?" then something is lost for those who need your help and your voice. Excessive humility is no virtue if it prevents us from acting.

—Elie Wiesel

---

**Example**

*The White Rose*, a student group in Nazi Germany during WWII, risked their lives to distribute leaflets and were eventually executed because of it. They did it not because it was popular, or convenient; they acted against the opinion of everyone else around them and still did the right thing—regardless of the consequences to themselves. They were convinced that they could make a difference, and they wanted to succeed. Considering the mounting self-destruction of Nazi Germany at the time, *not* doing anything would have been a much greater self-sacrifice—and for the wrong cause.

Biography—**Hans and Sophie Scholl**

Hans and Sophie Scholl were born in 1918 and 1921 in Ingersheim and Forchtenberg (Germany) respectively. While they were at first avid members of the Hitler Youth, they recognized that they had to position themselves against national socialism to prevent things from getting worse. This was due to their liberal and religious upbringing, the influence of messages from friends in the war, the reading of philosophical writings, listening to religious sermons, and their mentor Kurt Huber at the University of Munich. They started sending out a large number of fliers to the German public to explain to them the grave danger Germany was in. Ultimately, they were caught on February 18th, 1943. Only four days later they were sentenced to death by the notorious People's Court and executed the same day. After the war, they were regarded as important symbols of a German value-oriented resistance movement against the NS regime.

If we were to sacrifice our lives for a cause, what about all the people we could have helped if we had lived? What about the example we could have set for others during peaceful times? Are "good intentions" more important than the actual result? What, ultimately, is the measure of a hero? Is it possible for a successful businessperson to be a hero, or is this term reserved for those who stand up for others without recompense? Is social recognition the main motivator of heroism—an objective evaluation of one's accomplishments benefiting society—or is heroism an individual, objective description of a person relative to his *possibilities* and *decisions* and independent of his actual capabilities? Can only conflict bring out true heroes?

## 1.1.2 Heroes and Conflicts

Great heroes need great sorrows and burdens, or half their greatness goes unnoticed. It is all part of the fairy tale.

—Peter S. Beagle, *The Last Unicorn*

It is correct that true heroes remain mostly unrecognized in the absence of conflict. They are scattered among us. Like Atlas, from Greek mythology, they carry society on their shoulders—often anonymously yet gladly so, since they are faced with resentment and jealousy. In the novel *The Last Unicorn*, the unicorn is captured by a local carnival. The owner had to put a fake magical horn on the unicorn so that the people did not mistake her for a mare. While this describes a sad state of affairs, this idea also gives us hope. We should not take the world for what it appears to be. They might be difficult to find, but there are true heroes out there. As Peter S. Beagle put elegantly:

If men no longer know what they are looking at, there may well be other unicorns in the world yet, unknown and glad of it.

—Peter S. Beagle, *The Last Unicorn*

**Question**

Why should we not study philosophy as passive observers?

Heroes do not need evil in order to triumph; their only goal is a better world in which they want to live. A hero is not born out of a crisis or a single act of heroism. A crisis just puts the spotlight on some people. If only heroic acts in a crisis made heroes, every hero ultimately would work toward their own destruction: an ideal world without crises would not need such heroes. Based on that definition, in an ideal world, there would not be any heroes left. But heroism does not diminish when conditions in the world are improving. A hero does not work for a world in which his heroic traits are valued less and less; rather, he is dedicated to create a world in which he can develop himself (and others) better and better. For this reason, the opposite of a hero is not his opponent but, instead, the passive observer.

> **Idea**
>
> The opposite of a hero is not his opponent but, instead, the passive observer.

Often, a hero is someone who distinguishes himself from the crowd and rebels against obstacles, someone who does not follow society's standards, but instead acts according to universal, life-affirming values. It would be insufficient, however, to simply reject standards or follow certain tenets like "Love your neighbor." We need to know the *reason* that a certain rule is "good" and in which *context* it is applicable. We need to know why we should follow or reject a specific social standard. In order to recognize and evaluate the world, we need a foundation—a philosophy, the *Philosophy for Heroes*.

## 1.2 The Key to Wisdom

The wise man questions the wisdom of others because he questions his own, the foolish man, because it is different from his own.

—Leo Stein

I SEE MY PERSONAL KEY to wisdom as a form of the so-called "Socratic method." For me, the focal point is the conversation, whether in the form of an internal monologue or a discussion with others. The essential point is that there must be (at least) two sides so that we can reflect better on our own and the opposing position. This is important when thinking about "generally accepted truths," which, when addressed critically, can suddenly become the subject of a very emotional discussion. Trying to understand a different viewpoint by trying to defend it usually leads to a better understanding of your own viewpoint. We should be able to look beyond our normal ways of thinking, not regarding any subject as "untouchable" and therefore exempt from discussion. Often, you understand the original author's position and ideas only through his or her critics. They help to make clear what the author's position is *not*, improving the definition of what it *is*.

The physicist Richard Feynman was convinced that we should always contemplate the world from a new perspective. He asked, for example, how could it be that people in the Middle Ages believed in witches? What are our modern day "witches"? What views do we hold today without bothering to prove them? Every morning, millions of people around the world brush their teeth. But how do they know this has a positive effect on the health of their teeth? Or is it not obvious, that tooth brushing is beneficial? We know what our dentist has told us, but how does he know? Does he have evidence? No, he learned it during his education. But who was in charge of the curriculum?

The point is not to question tooth brushing but, as Feynman aimed to show, that we can and should question even obvious things. Through this, we achieve authentic progress because we are piercing through the self-supporting—possibly faulty—view of the majority. Likewise, we should be equally cautious of our own ingrained beliefs. If, confronted with an argument, we cannot come up with a counter-argument, we should halt the discussion there, take note of the argument, and write it down in order to examine it more closely later. Writing it down is particularly important in order to distance ourselves from the argument.

It is useless to continue the debate while fighting a losing battle. There is no way "around an argument" because it takes only a single valid argument to defeat a statement or even an entire position. Indeed, it is wise to play a discussion to "win," but in doing so we should not deceive ourselves. Should we later conclude that we were wrong, we should admit it and correct our position. It is interesting that such an action is often considered a "loss," as though the only important question is who had been right. We should ignore this and instead be pleased about having gained new insights.

When I disagree with a rational man, I let reality be our final arbiter; if I am right, he will learn; if I am wrong, I will; one of us will win, but both will profit.

—Ayn Rand, *For the New Intellectual*

Using books to research a topic, we should bear in mind that we may at some point lead a discussion or write an article about the topic. In doing so, we already reflect internally while reading, and follow the Socratic method, an internal dialog, which can lead us to an ideal learning experience.

I am apt to compare philosophical discussions to a game of chess. We start out in different positions; we have worked out a series of arguments, and we have some weak positions but also recognize weaknesses on our opponent's side. The goal is to find the opponent's core argument—the "king"—and refute it. In the opening, we declare our general arguments turn by turn and classify our opponent's views and arguments according to our textbook—our preconceptions. Unfortunately, most discussions end at this point since both parties often falsely assume they already know their opponent's side and no longer look at the board.

But only when we *deviate* from the textbook—the expected arguments of our opponent—does the "game" begin to progress, and by "attacking"—demanding clear definitions and categories—the first arguments are subdued. The loss of pieces is analogous to delving to a deeper philosophical level or into an investigation of the concepts. As long as one of the parties does not throw the pieces off the board and become abusive, as long as the discussion is not merely about questions concerning directly verifiable observations, and as long as both sides do not agree on a draw and settle their differences merely superficially, then every discussion—every game—will sooner or later end on fundamental philosophical questions about reality, or on the categorization of different terms—the "endgame." These are the questions whose answers create a ripple effect on all consequent philosophical positions, and which demonstrate the essential differences between both parties.

I have to add here, though, that most discussions actually are a *reversed* game of chess. Both sides usually start with their *conclusions* and end up with their openings, their initial basic views with which they went into the subject and developed their arguments. In addition, I have to add that the way of thinking and discussing that is described here is not shared by many people. Most discussions go through a number of linear arguments on the same level—and not on multiple levels of increasing abstraction.

A better approach might be to start with people from where they are and slowly build bridges from their point of view to ours. Do we want to "win" the discussion or do we want to effect change in the other person? We need to *listen* more and be alert to the underlying meaning. Usually, spoken words are rationalizations for underlying emotions rather than an expression of well-constructed philosophical positions. In addition, many people identify themselves with their own position; when we attack that position, then it is often falsely interpreted not as an attack on the philosophical position, but on the identity of the person. All we get from an attack is for the other person to hold *even more strongly* to his position. Instead, we need to begin with the idea that what the other person tells us is the logical result of the sum of his experiences, feelings, and knowledge. We have to assume that the other person tries to tell us the truth or at least some truth about his own person.

But this concept affects our daily routine as well, which we may be afraid to question because we fear that the results of our research could cause a guilty conscience and force us to change our ways. We not only shudder at the amount of effort future changes might require, but we also would have to face ourselves with a new awareness of our past and admit we have made mistakes. With enough time and determination, we can confront this psychological burden. But if we live and work in a group of people offering different perspectives, it is much easier to break free from a possible path of self-destruction.

Other than through a direct dialog, we can also achieve this kind of "mirror" by writing down our own thoughts. On paper, we can see the words we use, clearly and immutably. We need to think through how we formulate our words and how our own writing can then be understood, interpreted, or even refuted by others. It is a form of self-reflection when we let our written thoughts sit in a drawer for a while and "ripen." We thus enter into a dialog with the ideal counterpart: an older and hopefully wiser self.

 By painting the sky, Van Gogh was really able to see it and adore it better than if he had just looked at it. In the same way [...], you will never know what your husband looks like unless you try to draw him, and you will never understand him unless you try to write his story.

—Brenda Ueland, *If You Want to Write: A Book about Art, Independence and Spirit*

---

**Did you know?**

Though the title of the series is *Philosophy for Heroes*, we have to start—after this short introduction into the subject—from the bottom up and really get into the details. Take the following chapter as one in the course of the series; you will often come back to it for its definitions and more abstract ideas. While the topic of heroes will always accompany us in this book series, we will come back to it especially in the last book of the series where all the insights of each book will be summarized and developed.

⟶ Read more in *Philosophy for Heroes: Epos*

## 1.3 Why Philosophy Is Important

> In a few years, I must finish a certain work. I need not hurry myself; there is no good in that—but I must work on in full calmness and serenity, as regularly and concentratedly as possible, as briefly and concisely as possible.

—Van Gogh

---

**Question**

How is wishing to be in the spotlight on television similar to a *cargo cult*?

---

WITHOUT KNOWLEDGE OF philosophy and science—the future, where our views and technologies are going to lead us—*and* our (own and foreign) history (the past, how we have gotten to today's circumstances), we are living in an eternal present. A present that only exists—without a connection to a past that could possibly explain the present, and without a tomorrow that might develop from today.

What is left for people who are robbed of such standards (with which they could evaluate their situation) is only a glance at their current cultural environment, society, or a telescope into a different world—the media and its admiration of famous people. Although our culture is more likely to hold us in our own social position, television broadcasts the life of (seemingly) successful people. It does not show, however, what steps each celebrity had to take to get there.[1]

---

[1] cf. Dalrymple, *Life at the Bottom: The worldview that makes the underclass*, p. 70.

Thus, sometimes celebrities are seen as supernatural people. Without the knowledge of how to understand the world and how to build an existence, a life, and success in small steps, this appears, for this reason, like some kind of magic. It appears that if you only get your face on TV, success is going to automatically occur. Similar as to how heroic acts do not necessarily make a hero, someone who is celebrated as a hero does not necessarily become a better person.

It is a belief similar to the so-called "cargo cults" of the native inhabitants of the islands northeast of Australia. They built primitive runways and control towers in preparation for the Allied forces' aircrafts during and after World War II on which to land and unload valuable goods. Their execution seemed flawless to them, but they were missing something essential: cargo planes do not simply land because there is a runway. They are specifically ordered, loaded, and then sent to certain airports—with all parties involved being members of the Allies' international network of mutual trust, protection, and trade.

*Example*

Another example of a cargo cult is China under Mao Zedong. The state ordered the Five-Year Economic Plan of 1958, the "Great Leap Forward," in which large parts of the population were moved from working as farmers to producing steel. The idea was to achieve the economic success of industrialized nations by imitating some aspects, steel production being the most prominent factor at that time. Although China did produce massive amounts of steel, its quality was low grade, and it could hardly be sold on the world markets; the shift from agriculture to industry caused the biggest famine in human history.

The interaction in front of the camera, the building of runways, the steel production, or the gaining of knowledge are surely important goals in each individual realm. Alone, however, they do not lead to success, prosperity, or creativity. So if we want more than to copy others or maintain the status quo, but also create new things and, therefore, change the world by setting a living example, we have to understand the basic context. Understanding the basics, we can then, too, comprehend new and unknown situations. We do not only want to occupy ourselves with the past and what is known, but also prepare for the future. This requires knowledge of philosophy and the sciences.

> **Cargo cult •** A *cargo cult* refers to the behavior where some-one tries to imitate certain aspects of another (successful) person, expecting the same success. For example, celebrities are often on TV but just by managing to get yourself on TV, you will not nec-essarily become a celebrity.

This book, as well as philosophy in general, teaches the procedure to master problems and challenges, and to enable one to live a self-determined life. Just as in nature, where sensory cells have formed to react to external influences (instead of being pre-programmed), so it is that philosophy teaches humans *methods of thinking* to find answers to their questions concerning their lives.

Although numerous guidebooks have already been written on these topics, many times those offer just a series of personal accounts and general guidelines. What is missing is the broad foundation on which we can make the best decisions in a given situation—a foun-dation that connects our enthusiasm, values, and our inner world with rationality, science, and facts. Just like the pictures on televi-sion, it is, however, at a certain point no longer enough to be an example. For the distance between others and ourselves to not be-come too vast, we have to take our fellow man by the hand and climb new heights together. We need to learn to teach what we intuitively know and feel to be right.

[The book] aspires to be an invitation or introduction to philosophy for any lay person, most especially the young, wishing to learn something about this venerable intellectual tradition which started in Greece. I am addressing, above all, those who do not regard philosophy as being solely a venerable tradition but as a mode of thought that is still valid and can be of use when confronting their day-to-day problems. The main point is not to know how Socrates, twenty-five centuries ago, found a way of coping better with life in Athens, but to find a way of better understanding and enjoying life [today] ...

—Fernando Savater, *The Questions of Life*

But what are the questions with which we are confronted? Not all people can read and only a few read books on a regular basis. Is philosophy for this reason just a mind game for the rich and educated? What role does something like philosophy play in the life of an "ordinary" person?

The point is that *every* human carries a philosophy within him, upon which he either consciously or unconsciously acts. If not coming from one's own considerations, then such philosophy stems from family, the group, or the national culture. An individual's views are in turn fed by the ideas coming from the intellectuals—ideas that drip down to popular science books, schools, newspapers, and television. Contrary to production methods (and applied sciences to a lesser degree) which are under the constant scrutiny of market forces, these ideas spread mostly *unhindered*, as long as they are not questioned.

Such philosophical arguments are the result of thousands of hours of mental work of many scholars. Is it possible for someone who has never engaged in philosophy to build his own philosophical position or even go against opinions coming from universities? Probably, those people will glean their philosophical positions from their surroundings and imagine that they are independent of "those up there," and that others' ideas have no impact on them. But changes in the views of the general population almost always come from changes within the academic (or religious) sector. If you do not think for yourself, others will do the thinking for you. If a large portion of the population is not interested in philosophy, then a small number of philosophers will have a big impact on the entire population. People accept ideas that have "taken hold"—stayed unquestioned, that is. Therefore, it is even more important for anyone who is interested in philosophy to analyze current schools of thought and to actively get involved in the discussion, especially with the momentary trendsetters, and to make his or her voice heard.

[...] the ideas of economists and political philosophers, both when they are right and when they are wrong, are more powerful than is commonly understood. Indeed, the world is ruled by little else. Practical men, who believe themselves to be quite exempt from any intellectual influence, are usually the slaves of some defunct economist. Madmen in authority, who hear voices in the air, are distilling their frenzy from some academic scribbler of a few years back. I am sure that the power of vested interests is vastly exaggerated compared with the gradual encroachment of ideas.

—John Maynard Keynes, *The General Theory of Employment, Interest and Money*

Ayn Rand made a similar statement:

The uncontested absurdities of today are the accepted slogans of tomorrow. They come to be accepted by degrees, by dint of constant pressure on one side and constant retreat on the other—until one day when they are suddenly declared to be the country's official ideology.

—Ayn Rand, *The Return of the Primitive: The Anti-Industrial Revolution*

But why do we have to deal with *abstract* philosophical questions at all? Are there even questions beyond the political, economic, or scientific realm that are relevant to our lives? First it needs to be noted that knowledge is built upon a hierarchy. Answers to political, economic, and also scientific questions are found in association with answers coming from deeper levels of questions about human nature, logic, and even reality itself and how we perceive it. Most people merely lack self-confidence or courage to examine such questions; they ask themselves why exactly *they* should study and discuss philosophical teachings when thousands of others have already done so and supposedly confirmed them. As described earlier, philosophy is not subjected to direct examination like science studies are. Despite having a philosophy that conflicts with reality, we might not even realize it to be wrong (because we cannot see missed opportunities). We might realize it only when it is too late, as in the form of an inhumane system of government that was built on the very same flawed philosophy; or we might simply not know what it even means when a philosophy conflicts with reality.

Thus, it is up to each individual to decide whether to spend time studying philosophy or not. Joining leaders and using their success to measure the truthfulness of their philosophies appears to be a better alternative. But the difficulty here is to abstract someone else's concrete actions for general guidance for our own lives, or the reverse, connecting that person's lectures with his or her success; for that, we would need the very basics of philosophy we previously ignored. A person who has achieved wealth and power might have cheated his way to the top or simply was very lucky. Likewise, it does not necessarily mean that a person with lesser success is following a false philosophy or that the right philosophy would automatically lead to success.

Nevertheless, no matter how we twist and turn it, we do need a personal philosophical foundation to check how we should act. Despite having a grasp of this foundation, success is not guaranteed; you are not suddenly capable of moving mountains. But every new day, with each new decision, based upon accurate philosophy, we have a compass with which we can examine our direction at any given time. If we are moving in the right direction, although our steps might be very small, we can live in confidence that we are always getting closer to our goals. Contrary to everyday or temporary knowledge, a philosophy—even if it appears small and insignificant—influences each of us in every decision. An error in the foundation in our philosophy would be like having taken the wrong turn in a journey's beginning and finding yourself in the end at a totally different place than prospected. It is not important how fast you are moving but that you are making progress in the right direction.

## 1.4  Basics of Philosophy

F̲OR SOME READERS, many of the issues and items presented here might seem trivial. For example, it is obvious what "something" is and that it exists. Yet that is the very point and focus of these chapters, to have clean and clear definitions of what we are talking about. We are building up a new common language that all the readers of this series share, whatever their background. For this, we will approach the subject of philosophy by first dividing it into its components as follows:

- **Ontology**: *Where and what am I?*

- **Epistemology**: *How do I know?*

- **Ethics**: *What am I supposed to do?*

- **Esthetics**: *How can I concretize my ideal and what could I become?*

- **Politics**: *What may I do?*[2]

First, we will work on the foundation that we will then use for all subsequent chapters: ontology (axioms) and epistemology (sense perception, cognition, concepts, and knowledge). The central element in philosophy serves reality; hence, we will consider our basic assumptions and knowledge about the world. What do we know about the world and how can we organize this knowledge?

---

[2]In this book series, I will touch on the field of politics only occasionally.

**Did you know?**

"Ontology" derives from the Greek "onto" (which means "being") and "logio" (to study): the study of being. "Epistemology" comes from the Greek "episteme" (knowledge of") and means "the theory of knowledge."

Ontology and epistemology create the foundation for our ethics and even our esthetics. Only when we know what *is* and *how* we know it, can we start to think about what values are truly important for us (ethics) and how to represent those values as a reminder or motivator in the real world (esthetics).

$\longrightarrow$ Read more in *Philosophy for Heroes: Act*

Here, as well as during the course of this book series, we will interrupt our discussion again and again to define our terms. The idea is to create a common basis of communication. Words are empty if we have not come to an agreement on what they mean. Correspondingly, it is important to note that the terms and definitions for these concepts are just recommendations and serve as a clear distinction to other concepts. Ultimately, you might not agree with my definitions. But the idea is not to convince you to use them in this way, instead, they are offered for precise understanding of the text. We could just as well use different words, as is the case in different languages or ideologies. The point is that the concepts and definitions have to be distinct from each other and non-contradictory. In addition, we could imagine different concept definitions and hierarchies which are in themselves non-contradictory, but focus more on other aspects of reality.

> **ENTITY** • An *entity* is a "thing." Something that possesses an identity with properties (e.g., a plant produces oxygen, a stone has a hard surface, etc.).

**IDENTITY** • An *identity* is the sum total of all properties of an entity (e.g., weight: 160 pounds, length: 6 feet, has a consciousness, etc.).

**PROPERTY** • A *property* refers to the manner in which an entity (or a process) affects other entities (or other processes) in a certain situation (e.g., mass, position, length, name, velocity, etc.).

**CONFIGURATION OF A PROPERTY** • The *configuration of a property* relates to the intensity of a certain property of an entity.

**EFFECT** • An *effect* is the change caused to the configuration of the properties of an entity (e.g., the heating of water changes its temperature).

**Did you know?**

What many public discussions are *really* about is not the improvement of the concept in question, i.e. the question about the "correct" definition of a concept. Instead, they are about trying to capture a *term* whose corresponding concept already has a positive connotation in society. In the marketplace of ideas, people and organizations try to "sell" their ideas (good or bad) using trusted labels—just think of the many groups who call themselves "democratic."

⟶ Read more in *Philosophy for Heroes: Epos*

## 1.5  Ontology

I am, therefore I'll think.

—Ayn Rand, *Atlas Shrugged*

IN THE NATURAL SCIENCES, things and events of every kind are dissected into their parts and then separately surveyed and categorized. This categorization occurs irrespective of the individual observer. The scientist attempts to view the world from the outside. In doing so, he strives to eliminate or at least minimize his influence on the situation, trying to create an observer-independent model of reality.

---

**Did you know?**

Science is like a game. Not because it lacks seriousness, but because you have to follow strict rules if you want to partake in it. While there are other attempts of creating a system of rules to gain knowledge, the scientific method, with its prerequisite to document experiments and cite other works properly, has been the most useful and successful "set of rules" to gain knowledge about reality.

⟶ Read more in *Philosophy for Heroes: Continuum*

---

### 1.5.1 The Fallacy of the Stolen Concept

> When modern philosophers declare that axioms are a matter of arbitrary choice, and proceed to choose complex, derivative concepts as the alleged axioms of their alleged reasoning, one can observe that their statements imply and depend on "existence," "consciousness," "identity," which they profess to negate, but which are smuggled into their arguments in the form of unacknowledged, "stolen" concepts.
>
> —Ayn Rand, *Introduction to Objectivist Epistemology*

---

**Question**

Why can science not answer fundamental philosophical questions?

---

How far the scientific method has brought us until now is clearly visible in our everyday encounters with technology. But at the same time, we also see its limits when, for example, looking at questions of *free will*. The problem with this is that while science can point to physical parts of our cognition, our resulting consciousness is an indivisible *process* with a close linkage between observer and the object to be examined. It cannot be divided into its parts and separately examined. We cannot examine ourselves "from the outside." Introspection is by its very definition subjective.

**PROCESS** • A *process* describes the mechanism of a cause working to an effect (e.g., if you put an ice cube into a glass of water, the cooling of the water is the process).

**FREE WILL** • *Free will* refers to the faculty to be able to reflect on our cognition, i.e., to be not determined by external influences. The more one knows about and is aware of what influences him, the more free his will.

Applicable scientific experiments could possibly be found. But the problem would be evaluating results, if the supervising scientists have made use of these very elements they wanted to examine—those of free will—while conducting the experiment. Since these types of questions are essential to our understanding of the world, we require a *philosophical* foundation upon which science can, in turn, draw. We must first define what we understand by "knowledge" and how we can generate it.

---

### *Example*

If we developed a device that predicted our next decision, this device would fail when we used it ourselves: the knowledge of our next decision would influence our very next decision. Knowing what we would do, we could reflect upon our future decision once again. Depending on the person's mentality, they could decide against it, as a demonstration of their free will. Or, they could follow the "advice" and do exactly what the machine has told them to do. The latter effect is especially visible in political polls where people will tend to follow the majority (the so-called "bandwagon effect"). Likewise, on an individual level, the very act of getting analyzed or questioned might lead to an act of conformity. People tend to want to follow an authority (the device itself or the scientist that operates it), or want to be internally consistent and act according to their previous answers.

---

### Idea

Science is built upon a philosophical foundation, and thus is a branch of philosophy. Science cannot answer fundamental philosophical questions without violating its own scientific principles.

> **Question**
>
> Why is it important to study philosophy as a participant in the world and not just as a passive observer?

In contrast, most other philosophical schools of thought consider statements like "something exists" independent of the world, and consequently bring them into question. With his famous statement "I think, therefore I am," the philosopher and scientist René Descartes posited consciousness as a kind of basic truth (without also presupposing existence and the perception of reality) and from *that*, he inferred that we exist. While this solves the issue we had above with science, it raises new questions.[3] Is our *thinking*, in the first step, independent of our existence?

The underlying mistake of the notion of a consciousness existing independent of reality, which considers the world "from outside," is what Ayn Rand describes as the *fallacy of the stolen concept*. It states that argumentation against an idea constitutes a contradiction if we have presupposed that very idea in the argument.[4] In the case of our example of the question of existence, the error simply lies therein, that we cannot call existence into question without presupposing the very same existence—we certainly must exist in order to question it. So, here, we do not try to look at ourselves from the outside as a first step and only then deduce our existence. Instead, we accept that we are part of and are interacting with reality. Suppositions born of themselves, floating "outside of time and space," have no place.

---

[3]Descartes' approach is called *rationalism*, the notion that we could follow everything by simply thinking (see Chapter 1.6.4, "Rationalism").

[4]Implicitly or explicitly, meaning it does not matter if we have not expressed the idea directly.

> **Idea**
>
> The essence of philosophy is to understand yourself as being
> part of reality, rather than isolating yourself from reality as
> a passive observer.

**FALLACY OF THE STOLEN CONCEPT** • The *fallacy of the stolen
concept* refers to the fact that in the refutation of a statement, the
statement itself cannot (implicitly or explicitly) be a part of the
refutation. We cannot argue against our existence because the
act of arguing presupposes that very existence.[5]

This is one of the cornerstones of Rand's approach to philosophical
arguments. We first have to examine a statement or question—especially in regard to the fallacy of the stolen concept—and challenge
its assumptions before proceeding to evaluate or answer it. It should
be emphasized that this way of finding the truth deals with neither
a purely rationalistic nor a purely empirical procedure. For the acquisition of knowledge, sense perception is just as necessary as a
logical integration. Without integrated sense perceptions, there is
no understanding of axioms. Without axioms, there can be no logic.
Without logic, there is no integration of sense perceptions.[6]

---

[6]cf. Peikoff, *Objectivism: The Philosophy of Ayn Rand*, pp. 4–12.

## 1.5.2 The Axiom of Existence

> **AXIOM** • An *axiom* is a self-evident truth (e.g., "Something exists").

A "self-evident" truth refers to a statement that justifies itself through its existence. For example, "This sentence exists," is a *self-evident statement*. If it were not put down in writing or expressly said (if it did not exist), then it would not comprise a statement and thus could not be false. In contrast, if it *is* put down in writing, and read or expressly said (it exists), it is correct, and thus, self-evident.

> **SELF-EVIDENT STATEMENT** • A *self-evident statement* is a statement whose reasoning is contained within itself (e.g., the establishment of the axiom of existence necessitates the very same existence).

> **AXIOM OF EXISTENCE** • The *axiom of existence* states that something *exists*. Without existence, there would be no entities. Particularly, there would be no interactions between entities, no perception, and, for this reason, no knowledge; a line of reasoning for this axiom would not be possible.

Above, we have discussed that we cannot reason that we exist because we can think about our existence. At the same time, we *think* when we contemplate about our existence. So, what comes first, consciousness or existence? What truths can we rely on in philosophy? We could write down any number of such self-evident truths. However, the point here is not the exact wording, but its meaning. It is not only about the sentence, "This sentence exists," but also about reading and understanding it. So, we become conscious about the sentence (its existence) and its meaning (its identity). Thus, the answer is that *none* of these elements (existence, identity, and consciousness) stands "first," but that all are true at the same time. This insight will accompany us throughout this chapter. We will see that there really is just one single self-evident truth. Thus, the question about the sequence of the truths is of no concern.

Certainly no one is *forced* to accept a self-evident statement. Who nevertheless denies the foundation of knowledge, and places himself on a pedestal and grandly proclaims that we live in a chaotic universe, whose properties we are not capable of identifying, accepts exactly the assumptions about the world against which he tries to argue: the *existence* of reality (especially his own existence) and his *consciousness*, with the help of which he can become aware of the *identity* of the real world. The only resulting alternative to the acceptance of the axioms and the objectivity of reality we would be left with is, therefore, silence; whoever does not make or process any statements cannot entangle himself in his statement or in a contradiction.

### 1.5.3 The Axiom of Identity

If something *exists*, then there is *something* that exists. Entities thus have a definite identity, which leads us directly to a new axiom:

> **AXIOM OF IDENTITY** • The *axiom of identity* states that *something* exists. Without this axiom, "entities" could *possibly* exist, but they would have no identity and, for this reason, would likewise possess no properties. In such a reality, it follows that no perception or knowledge would be possible either; particularly, we could not form arguments against the axiom of identity: without identity, statements in general would be impossible because they, too, would have no identity—no statement. In Objectivism, this axiom is also designated as "*A* is *A*": every identity has *definite* properties and no others.

**Question**

What is the nature of the identity of an entity?

Because of this *axiom of identity*, contradictions in reality thus cannot exist. Everything that exists has definite (and not indeterminate or undefined) properties so that we can distinguish between an entity $A$ and another entity *not-A*. Causality thus follows from this: i.e., each entity behaves according to its properties. Every entity, therefore, possesses a number of properties that are free of contradiction, along with which properties of the same type may be attributed, so long as they are not different. An entity cannot at the same time take on two different masses or velocities, and an entity cannot at the same time be visible and invisible.

---

**Idea**

Entities have exactly one (specific and distinct) identity at any given time.

---

**Question**

Can contradictions exist in reality if we can imagine them?

---

A line of reasoning against this principle is brought up time and again in discussions—specifically, that we could imagine contradictions with our minds. We could *imagine* jumping onto the moon, or that "1 = 2." If contradictions could exist in our heads, could they not then also be part of reality, and would we not have to renounce our claims concerning the use of logic?

Here, the point is that what we imagine in these examples is not actually contradictory. Jumping onto the moon—assuming the technology exists—may be completely possible. So what we imagine is either: not ourselves as we are (but ourselves with muscles that function in a particular way), or ourselves but in a world without gravity. What we particularly *cannot* imagine are direct contradictions that violate the Axiom of Identity. We could strain ourselves and think hard about a pink, invisible unicorn. In a "non-objective reality," entities would possess no identity, i.e., something could also be something else. An entity could simultaneously be completely black and white, visible and invisible, here and there.

The crucial error in such a line of reasoning is the confusion of *object A* and the *illusion of A*, which ultimately constitute two different entities. Of course, we can write down the equation "$1 = 2$" and make a picture of it. But what this equation expresses, for example, "two apples are one apple," is *not* realizable.

## 1.5.4  The Axiom of Consciousness

Through the *contemplation* of reality, and with the help of our *intellect*, we have now been able to *discover* the two axioms of existence and identity. But we are not the scientists mentioned earlier, who could discover truths about the world without regard to them being *part* of that very same world. We became conscious about the two axioms on our own. The prerequisite for the comprehension of the world is our *consciousness*:

> **CONSCIOUSNESS** • With our *consciousness*, we can become conscious about something, therefore, it is the *process* that emerges from the faculty of an entity to reflect on and to perceive oneself and other entities and their properties (cognition).

> **AXIOM OF CONSCIOUSNESS** • The *axiom of consciousness* states that we can become aware of our existence, our identity, and the external world.

A denial of this axiom would imply that through the act of denying, we were conscious of at least a part of reality. Having consciousness and at the same time denying having it would be a contradiction. Thus, it is not possible to argue consistently against the notion that we have a consciousness.

---

**Did you know?**

Ontology is actually just a part of the larger field of *metaphysics*. Besides ontology, it also includes questions like:

- "What is the origin of the universe?"
- "How is there something rather than nothing?"
- "Could the universe be different?"
- "What is free will?"

$\longrightarrow$ Read more in *Philosophy for Heroes: Continuum*

---

## 1.6 Epistemology

> [Ontology] and epistemology are simultaneous—what exists
> and how we know it are the foundation that starts together.
> And that's why the very first axiom is "Existence exists, and
> the act of grasping this implies there is something, and we
> have the faculty for being aware of it." And thereafter we
> shift back and forth, "We have consciousness," "*A* is *A*," "Ex-
> istence is independent of consciousness," "We acquire knowl-
> edge by reason," and so on. [Ontology and epistemology] are
> completely intertwined.

—Leonard Peikoff, *Understanding Objectivism*

WITH ONTOLOGY, we were able to realize that we can be conscious of reality. With epistemology, we want to discuss *how* we
can be conscious of reality. It is important to note here that "axioms
are *preconditions* of knowledge; they are not the starting points of a
deductive development; they are not the foundations from which we
infer conclusions à la mathematics. [...] If all you know is 'Existence
exists,' and you sit and stare at that, you will never get any further.
Those axioms are the foundations of knowledge, which means they
*enable* us then to look at reality, to have actual experience that we
then have to conceptualize, induce, integrate, and so on."[7]

---

**Question**

Why are ontology and epistemology simultaneous?

---

[7] Peikoff, *Understanding Objectivism*, p. 283.

Besides ontology, epistemology is a supporting foundation of philosophy and concerns itself with how knowledge can be acquired and validated. In that regard, it is important to note that just because we have started with the axioms (ontology), this does not mean that ontology stands first in a long chain of deductions and conclusions. We have to correct our hierarchical list of philosophical elements and replace it with a structure with mutual dependencies (see Figure 1.1).

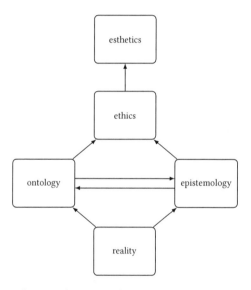

**Figure 1.1:** Ontology and epistemology are not derived from each other, instead they *together* form the foundation of ethics.

**Idea**

Ontology and epistemology are simultaneous—what exists and how we know it form a foundation of philosophy.

The implications of this insight are far-reaching. If we look at *how* we get to know something (epistemology) as a *corollary* from the axioms, we could never find out what our consciousness, our mind, and our will is. These concepts would become something undefined, and we would not be able to recognize other entities with a consciousness as such. Only with other people could we argue that, because they are similar to us, they likewise must have a consciousness. Animal, artificial or alien intelligences would always be beings without consciousness.

## 1.6.1  Perception

 Man's senses are his only direct cognitive contact with reality and, therefore, his only source of information. Without sensory evidence, there can be no concepts; without concepts, there can be no language; without language, there can be no knowledge and no science.

—Ayn Rand, *Philosophy: Who Needs It*

Our perceptual faculty is the filtering, integration, and association of several sense perceptions which were converted to a form usable by our *cognition* (so-called *sense data*). For example, if we hold an apple in our hand, we see its color and feel its shape and surface. And if we look at it, our eyes provide us with a pre-processed image of the apple that includes edge-detection using the contrast between the apple and the background. These sense data are combined, resulting in our *sense perception* of the apple. Sense data is information, converted to a form usable by the cognitive process, about an effect registered by a *sense organ* (e.g., an eye, a nose, an ear, etc.). A sense organ is an entity that is connected to another entity with cognition, and that can register effects of different intensities of properties.

**Sense organ** • A *sense organ* is an entity (e.g., an eye, a nose, an ear, etc.) that is connected to another entity with cognition, and that can register effects of different intensities of properties.

**Sense data** • *Sense data* is information, converted to a form usable by cognition, about an effect registered by a sensory organ.

**Sense perception** • Our perceptual faculty is the filtering, and association of sense data. This happens automatically with our sensory organs. Further filtering and association of those *sense perceptions* happens during the cognitive process (our consciousness).

**Qualia** • The individual instances of conscious experience of sense data are called *qualia.*

**Self-reference (recursion)** • If a statement or a process *references itself,* it is called *recursion.* Examples would be "Read the sentence you are now reading again" (recursive statement), two opposing mirrors in which the images mirror until infinity (recursive process), cell division where a new cell is created that divides itself as well (likewise a recursive process), etc.

**Cognition** • *Cognition* is the faculty for processing and correcting qualia, generating and applying knowledge, changing preferences, as well as reflecting on the process of cognition itself. The result of the process of cognition is consciousness.

**Perception** • *Perception* is the whole process of sense perception combined with cognition.

---

**Question**

Which five issues could have a detrimental effect on our objective perception?

To understand the context, it is helpful to look at the whole process of *cognition*, from the sense data to the knowledge we gain. Fundamentally, we can divide it into seven steps (see Figure 1.2):

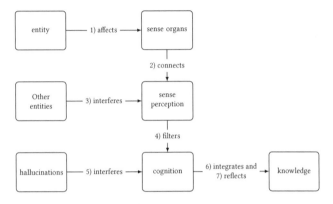

**Figure 1.2:** Process of cognition

1. **Effect on the observer by the entity that is being perceived.** Entities affect us independent of our perception. While we *say* that we look *at* something, that we are *actively* taking a look *at* something, the effect of the entity (e.g., light rays) reaches us without any effort or interference on our part. This is similar to what we have discussed previously in Chapter 1.5, "Ontology." First, reality exists, then we can become aware of it. Concerning philosophy, this view is the so-called "rationalism." Ultimately, there is confusion between our ability to actively focus and filter our sense perception, and the passive registering of the effects of other entities. Just because we have the ability to wear "rose-colored glasses" and to see only good in the world, this does not change the world—only our evaluation of it.

2. **Processing of the effect with our senses.** The sense data are combined into a complete sense perception. Any processing within our sense organs happens dependent on the differ-

ent individual sense organs. The same picture or the same sound is processed by the sense organs of different people in different ways (e.g., red-green colorblindness) and correspondingly different sense data is being provided to the process of cognition (consciousness).

3. **Interference of other entities.** If other entities affect our sense organs, our sense perception could be distorted. Additional unrelated information from our environment has (noise) to be filtered.

4. **Filtering.** Our consciousness is limited; we filter the incoming sense data and focus on a specific part. Because of this necessarily limited perception, we could overestimate or overlook certain sense data. These *qualia* are by their definition subjective, as the consciousness of every human is unique.

5. **Hallucinations.** Our brain could misinterpret or create false sense perceptions. Then we could mistake, for example, dreams or hallucinations induced by sleep deprivation or drugs as objective sense data from the outside. Suffering from schizophrenia, you could even end up misinterpreting your own *thoughts* as sense data coming from the outside.

6. **Processing of the sense data.** With our consciousness having become aware of the sense data as qualia (as subjective experiences), we integrate and categorize them using logic. In this process, errors could happen, be it because of sloppiness, laziness, or because of an erroneous philosophy. For example, with the assumption that "All humans read *Philosophy for Heroes* (and Max is a human)," the conclusion "Max reads *Philosophy for Heroes*" would be logically correct, but (unfortunately) the assumption would be wrong with regard to content. On the other hand, the assumption "Readers of *Phi-*

*losophy for Heroes* are humans (and Max is a human)" is correct with regard to content, but a conclusion like "Max reads *Philosophy for Heroes*" would not be necessarily logically correct. Just because he is a human, that does not mean he reads this book.

**Did you know?**

Philosophy knows a long list of logical fallacies. If we learn and practice evading them in our own speech, not only will we become more honest, but we can also become much more aware when others try to use them to manipulate us.

$\longrightarrow$ Read more in *Philosophy for Heroes: Act*

7. **Reflection.** In order to interpret our conscious subjective experiences (qualia), correct errors, and draw conclusions about reality, we have to reflect on the cognitive process. Reflection itself is also part of cognition—we also have to *reflect on how we reflect*. If we assume that our environment has been conspiring against us, we question everything but our own paranoia. But we would also have to check whether our assumption about our environment is correct. A special case of (missing) reflection is if you are fine with the fact that you never reach a conclusion when using a recursive statement for an argument. With a statement like, "I cannot make statements," you would never reach a conclusion if you try to rectify it by saying "I cannot make statements except for the statement, 'I cannot make statements.'" You could do that for infinity. It is like saying that "something is true because because because ..." without ever providing a final argument why it is true.

**Did you know?**

Psychological influence through marketing, political propaganda, terror, or cults prefers to target our ability to judge and reflect. It is much easier to influence how somebody interprets and processes information than to influence the material world itself and find supporting facts which might not exist in the first place.

⟶ Read more in *Philosophy for Heroes: Act*

For the last point, reflection, we have to expand our discussion a little bit. We have now discussed how we can perceive the world and how an individual, subjective experience of reality is created in our consciousness (qualia). At the same time, we have also listed what problems can occur during the process of sense perception and cognition, i.e., how our view of the world can be distorted. Ultimately, it looks as if we had indeed *one* experience of the world but could (with the exception of the axioms, the foundations of knowledge) not be sure that what we perceive really corresponds to the real world.

But what is the qualitative difference compared to our discussion of axioms? We know that *something* has had an effect on us, we just do not know how, what, and from where exactly. It is like a murder-mystery game, where we have to track down the effect step by step to its original source; we have to reflect on the whole process of cognition. If we know that our conversation partner lies, we can process the information we get from him in a way so that the lie no longer has power over us. Or when we look at a spoon in a glass of water, it looks as if it is bent. But our experience or our knowledge about light refraction tells us that it is not the spoon but the light that is "bent." So, the more we know about what distorts our cognition, the more our insights relate to reality.

Ultimately, reflection is a loop, because new knowledge might also shine new light on our existing knowledge of the workings of our own cognition, which again could change our perception of the world, which again might provide us new insights into our cognition, and so forth. While we are not born with knowledge about the world or our cognition, we do not have to know how our cognition works in order for it to work. Our mind has the *automatic* ability to learn and to use basic logic, i.e., to associate two different sense perceptions to form a single conscious experience. When we see a barking dog, we can quickly learn that it really is the dog that is barking by combining our visual with our auditory sense data.

Obviously, we can spin it further at this point and argue that we could be wrong in the assessment of our cognitive abilities and that we are unable to check them because our cognitive abilities are defective. This could end up with us having a blind spot in regard to certain aspects of reality, especially if we add outside manipulation. We cannot easily refute thought experiments where we are nothing but brains in a laboratory of a mad scientist, or more generally, where the universe actively conspires against us and deliberately feeds us wrong information into our mind.

**Did you know?**

The idea that reality is an illusion is a popular notion, going back to "Plato's cave"—an allegory by Plato to show that we could mistake what we see as mere shadows of what reality really is. It is also a central motif of *Matrix*, a movie that challenges the viewer to ask whether we live in a computer simulation. The point is that we *can* always find out—eventually. In all cases, it is impossible to shield the inside world from the "jitter" of the outside world without leaving evidence.

⟶ Read more in *Philosophy for Heroes: Continuum*

### 1.6.1.1 The Limits of Perception

> Man is neither infallible nor omniscient; if he were, a discipline such as epistemology—the theory of knowledge—would not be necessary nor possible: his knowledge would be automatic, unquestionable, and total.

—Ayn Rand, *Introduction to Objectivist Epistemology*

**Question**

What, if any, effect on us must remain hidden?

For now, we assume we are living in a universe that does not try to actively deceive us. With this condition, can we perceive reality objectively, as it is, or are we principally limited? Objective perception relates to the faculty to perceive any properties of any entity *in principle*, independent of one's own individual sense organs. For this, we need cognition, the faculty of processing and correcting sense perceptions, and generating and applying knowledge. Without cognition, the following two objections could be raised:

- Our sense organs themselves could be inadequate to perceive certain aspects of reality.

- Certain identities could categorically elude sense perception, or besides their identities which we perceive, entities could possess a deeper "identity-in-itself" which we could not perceive.

Let us first look at the question whether our senses might be so limited that we perhaps *fundamentally* cannot perceive a part of reality. What about infrared or ultraviolet radiation, ultrasound, electromagnetism, infrasound, or Earth's magnetic field, for example? We lack the necessary sense organs for these sources of information. In contrast, a closed, non-transparent box is no obstacle for a dolphin: while a direct view of the contents is hidden from its eyes, its brain extends its spatial perception of the world by means of sonar, and the box becomes virtually transparent.[8]

In spite of our limitations, we can, however, make objective perceptions. As discussed above, perception consists of the sense perception of the actual sense data (the interaction of a signal with one's sense organs) as well as the cognitive processing with one's mind. We are thus not limited to direct effects on our senses, but we can also incorporate indirect effects into our thoughts. For example, we could construct devices (e.g., a camera with color translation, a compass, or special microphones) which would allow us to recognize these signals with one of our other senses, or we could communicate with animals that possess these sense organs (e.g., with dogs, owing to their sense of smell). So, any entity can be perceived as it interacts by definition with other entities. And ultimately, given enough time, as effects result in yet other effects, everything is interrelated with everything else.

**Idea**

We can overcome physical limitations of our senses through the use of our minds and scientific instruments. No effect on us necessarily needs to remain hidden.

---

[8]cf. White, *In Defense of Dolphins: The New Moral Frontier*, p. 26.

### 1.6.1.2 The Range of Perception

Now, what's the difference between an invisible, incorporeal, floating dragon who spits heatless fire and no dragon at all? If there's no way to disprove my contention, no conceivable experiment that would count against it, what does it mean to say that my dragon exists?

—Carl Sagan, *The Demon-Haunted World: Science as a Candle in the Dark*

> **Question**
>
> How should we deal with arbitrary claims?

Assume for a moment that there was something that did not interact with the entities in our reality, and thus was not recognizable through observation, either directly or indirectly (i.e., through its reaction with other entities, such as machines). To what extent should we attribute this "something" to reality? If it cannot react with anything, then it can have no effect. And without an effect, the entity has no properties. It could "exist" in a formal sense but would have no identity.[9] Such a "something" would have no connection to reality. We could classify this "something" in the same category as invisible, weightless dragons.

The argument remains that such entities would possibly possess properties of some kind that we simply have not yet discovered. The problem here is that, theoretically, there could be an infinite number of such entities. To what extent we attach a *value* to these entities is a question of *ethics*. In the first place, a life-oriented philosophy *de-*

---

[9]To clear up any confusion: "something" without an identity does not exist.

nies the existence of anything for which there is no evidence, since we cannot take into consideration all these possible entities with every decision we make. But the fact that we are limited is not the reason we, in our actions, deny or ignore arbitrary claims about the existence of undiscovered entities. We are ignoring such claims because they are not proper claims. Just because you claim something, it does not mean that there is any merit to it, or that we have to actively ignore it in our decisions. We consider only claims or arguments that have some connection to reality.

---

**Did you know?**

Here, you could ask of course: "What about God?" But "God" is no trivial concept that can be explained with identity and existence. For the discussion, we have to clear up a whole set of other points first. If you are impatient...

⟶ Read more in *Philosophy for Heroes: Epos*

---

Immanuel Kant went one step further in *Prolegomena*. He denied that people have the capability of recognizing the "things in themselves:"

> There are things given to us as objects of our senses existing outside of us yet we know nothing of them as they may be in themselves, but are acquinted only with their appearances, i.e., with the representations that they produce in us because they affect our senses.

—Immanuel Kant, *Prolegomena to Any Future Metaphysics: That Will Be Able to Come Forward as Science*[10]

---

[10]Kant and Hatfield, *Prolegomena to Any Future Metaphysics: That Will Be Able to Come Forward as Science*, pp. 40–41.

The problem of the "things in themselves" is an extension of the problem of the "invisible dragon." He understood it as everything of an entity which could not be perceived in principle. In practice, this would mean that every perceivable entity was or could be linked to a non-perceivable entity. But these "things in themselves" would have no properties and thus also no identity and according to their definition would not exist.

In the Middle Ages, people wrote "Here be dragons" on all places of maps outside of their geographical knowledge. Today, such signs still exist, despite having satellites and the Internet. But it is the maps of the mind that still carry such signs. People say that everything in the world has already been discovered and that there is nothing more to do for explorers and adventurers. I point them to those *mental* maps that are still filled, yes, with "dragons"—but more importantly, also with opportunities.

The universe is probably littered with the one-planet graves of cultures which made the sensible economic decision that there's no good reason to go into space—each discovered, studied, and remembered by the ones who made the irrational decision.

—Randall Munroe, *Xkcd*

**Idea**

Arbitrary claims can be ignored. Just because you can make the claim does not mean that it has any connection to reality that needs to be considered.

It lies with adventurers and researchers to take on the risk of traveling into the unknown, to discover and map out these unfamiliar worlds; the burden of proof rests on them, but so, too, does the glory of their possible discovery. For them, their pursuit of knowledge is an ethical question. But while they do not know *what* is at their goal, they know there is *something*. Sure, there is the possibility of finding a treasure island, but they do not travel there exclusively to prove or disprove that unsubstantiated claim. Even if all they find is the sea, their discovery would still be worth something, namely filling the map, showing others so they do not have to search for themselves.

So, objective perception does not mean that we would possess sense organs that automatically supply us with "correct" information from the environment. Rather, we are in the position to extract objective information about reality from the environment, with or without means of assistance, but in any case with the assistance of the *mind*. Objective perception means that we can draw conclusions about the causes of everything that interacts with our bodies (more precisely, our senses). When we see a ray of light, we cannot automatically know its source. We need a series of subsequent light rays in order to construct a three-dimensional image of our surroundings. In addition, we still require conscious knowledge about possible optical illusions and hallucinations of the brain. If we have correctly processed all this knowledge, we obtain an objective picture of reality. Here it should again be emphasized what we previously have established: without objective perception, the logical discussion of perception itself is ultimately not possible in the first place. To claim that our perception is subjective would again be a fallacy of the stolen concept. If we had no possibility of perceiving the world, we could acquire no knowledge, including knowledge of the axioms.

## 1.6.2 Concepts

> If names are correct, there is order; if names are allowed to become confused, there is disorder. What causes the confusions of names are explanations that involve an excess of elegance and subtlety. If explanations involve such excesses, then the not-acceptable is called the acceptable, the not-so is called so, the incorrect is called correct, and the not-wrong is called wrong.

—Lü Bu We, *The Annals of Lü Buwei*

Now we know how our process of perception works. But we are not an infinite video recorder which saves all perceptions one after the other. In addition, the universe itself is potentially infinite (or at least very large). But our consciousness possesses an identity and, for this reason, is finite. How can we then grasp a potential infinite amount of information with our finite mind?

A solution to this problem is *concepts*. Concepts are abstractions that permit us a description of reality and allow us to form compact units of information from many different origins, which can then be processed by our short-term memory. For our further progress, we first consider a list of fundamental concepts as a kind of reference basis. Figure 1.3 and Figure 1.4 illustrate an overview of, and context for, the concepts listed below. Here we see, in particular, the interdependencies governing them.

**CATEGORY** • A *category* is the mental correlation between entities.

**CONCEPT** • A *concept* is a category that is delineated by a definition, and determined by the nature of the entity.

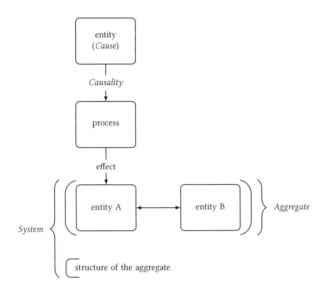

**Figure 1.3:** Overview of definitions (systems)

**Cause** • A *cause* refers to the entity that has or had an effect on another entity (e.g., the ice cube in the glass is the cause for the drink having gotten cold).

**Causality** • *Causality* refers to the effect of one or several entities on another entity in a certain situation (e.g., an accident is no random occurrence, there are one or several causes which led to the accident, such as lack of sleep, a technical defect, poor visibility, etc.).

**Aggregate** • An *aggregate* is a number of entities that have a reciprocal effect on one another, so that they can be considered collectively as their own entity (e.g., a cup full of water—all water molecules interact with each other).

**Structure** • A *structure* is a description of required properties, dependencies, and arrangement of a number of entities (e.g., cube-shaped).

**System** • A *system* is an aggregate with a definite structure (e.g., an ice cube, the axioms, etc.).

**Pointer** • A *pointer* can be a word, picture, gesture, etc. that "points" to one or more entities. It can be used in their place, e.g., if you "point" to a specific apple by saying "this apple," you do not have to actually take the apple in your hand to make it clear about which apple you are speaking.

**Term** • A *term* is the name of a concept (e.g., as a word or fixed word combination, such as "goods and services" or "in a jiffy"). Every concept has a term pointing to it, but not every term is a concept (e.g., conjunctions like "and").

**Definition** • A *definition* is the possible demarcation of a number of entities by means of perceptions, concepts, and axioms (e.g., grass is a "plant," a "living organism" which uses "photosynthesis.") It consists of a list of properties and processes of entities(cf. Rand, Binswanger, and Peikoff, *Introduction to Objectivist Epistemology*, pp. 71–74) in question.

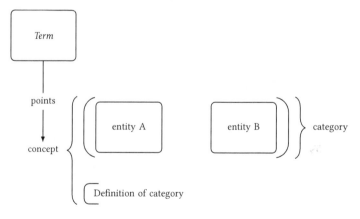

**Figure 1.4:** Overview of *definitions* (concepts)

**INTEGRATION** • *Integration* is the classification of perceived entities into one or several concepts, as well as classification of existing concepts into more general concepts or a concept hierarchy (e.g., the classification of a perceived sound wave as a definite word, or classification of the concept "human" into the more general concept "life-form").

**CONTRADICTION** • A *contradiction* can result from a (possibly erroneous) logical integration. This becomes visible when the corresponding concept has a property while *not having* it at the same time (such as an invisible pink unicorn, boiling ice, a full empty cup, etc.).

**LOGIC** • *Logic* is the method of non-contradictory integration of knowledge or perceptions.

**KNOWLEDGE** • *Knowledge* constitutes sense data, logically integrated perceptions, concepts, or concept hierarchies. It can also be created from logically integrated conclusions from existing knowledge.

---

Biography—**Aristotle**

Aristotle lived around 384 to 322 BC in ancient Greece and was a naturalist and philosopher. He is considered the founder of Western philosophy and sciences and a proponent of this world, our reality. Though a pupil of Plato, he discarded Plato's theory of forms; instead, he propagated the view that reality consists only of entities that can be perceived, and that concepts, thoughts, and imaginations themselves have no properties and do not exist on their own. According to Aristotle, entities act according to their nature and the world is not a shadow of a "divine dimension." It exists on its own—perceivable and intelligible by the human mind.

### 1.6.2.1 Concept Formation

When faced with new perceptions, we might have to form new concepts and definitions. As described previously, a concept involves a mental connection of entities, which is described by a definition and determined by the common nature of the entities. So we consider not just the effect of a single entity through *measurements*, but instead abstract and connect sense data perceived from an entire series of entities. This abstraction is achieved by enumerating only the *common* properties of the entities and *omitting* the measurements of the entities. For instance, we observe blue, yellow, and red ball-shaped entities. Instead of creating separate concepts for each color, we form the concept "ball" with the property "color." The configurations of the property—the colors blue, yellow, and red—no longer appear in the definition of the concept. Basically, this corresponds to the aforementioned reflection of our individual experiences of our consciousness (qualia).

**Idea**

Concepts are generated through the omission of measurements.

*Example*

When we have selected our concepts properly, we do not have to adapt them even when making surprising new discoveries. A famous example pertains to swans. Just because we have only seen white swans does not necessarily mean that "whiteness" is a substantial property of the definition of a swan. Color is a property, black and white feathers constitute a measurement. If we find a black swan, we can reuse the concept of a swan, using black instead of white for the property of color.

**Question**

How do concepts increase our mental capacity?

Our new knowledge of concepts can also be applied in reverse. Assuming we have defined our concepts properly, we know that two balls of different colors will roll the same way down a slanted surface. Rolling is a behavior related to its shape, not color. So instead of having to run two separate experiments and to describe the process of rolling for each individual color, we can predict the behavior for a ball of *any* color with the definition of a single concept.

**Idea**

With the aid of concepts, we can make statements about the behavior of a large number of entities without having to consider them individually. This way, we increase our mental capacities multifold.

### 1.6.2.2 Establishment of a Definition

"See how *bad* a story you can write. See how dull you can be. Go ahead. That would be fun and interesting. I will give you ten dollars if you can write something thoroughly dull from beginning to end!" And of course, no one can.

—Brenda Ueland, *If You Want to Write: A Book about Art, Independence and Spirit*

---

**Question**

Definitions do not need to be complete; what is their role?

---

Concepts always encompass *all* properties of the entities, regardless of which definition we give them at the moment. In contrast, for a definition, not all properties must necessarily be specified. We do not have to be omniscient to provide a proper definition. In the majority of cases, definitions are incomplete. But at a minimum, definitions should differentiate their associated concepts from other similar concepts. The reason for an incomplete definition could be that we simply have not yet discovered all properties of a concept. Without the presence of another concept that overlaps with the definition of our concept, a complete definition is not necessary.[11]

---

**Idea**

Definitions do not need to be complete; they simply must be able to clearly separate concepts from one another.

---

[11] cf. Rand, Binswanger, and Peikoff, *Introduction to Objectivist Epistemology*, p. 99.

Figure 1.5 shows the perception of three circles of different sizes, from which we define the concept "circle" with the property "radius." As long as we have seen only gray circles, the definition of "circle" and "gray circle" would be identical. If we make subsequent perceptions of circles of different colors, we can then add the property of color. With our initially limited perceptions, the original definition was correct, in the sense that it correctly encompassed all existing perceptions. With subsequent perceptions, it was necessary to broaden our definition of the existing concept and add the color property.

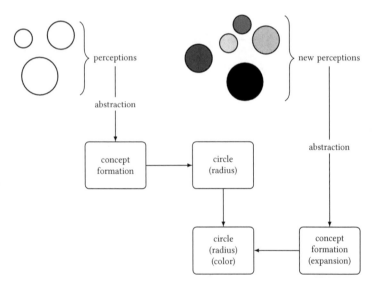

**Figure 1.5:** Example of the broadening of a definition through specialization due to new perceptions

Not every concept, however, is suited to help with the comprehension of the world. For example, there are concepts with contradictory properties ("round rectangle"), concepts which represent enumerations ("all horses and pigs"[12]), and concepts which depend di-

---

[12]We should instead find out the underlying common properties or henceforth treat them as

rectly on the results of measurements ("blue horses"[13]). Ultimately, just because we can write down a definition of a concept, this does not mean that it is necessarily a valid concept.

I want to emphasize here that concepts do not, as Plato believed, "inhere" in an entity. Thus, no "person-concept" resides within a person. Concepts themselves are not entities or properties. Instead, they are *pointers* to categories. They concern purely mental constructs, with whose help we try to abstract and simplify nature to the point that we can apply them productively. They thus depend on our situation, our knowledge of the world, and our needs. To what extent they help us in life naturally depends on the degree to which they are free of contradictions in their construction, whether we have correctly integrated our perceptions, and whether we have made sensible decisions in separating the concepts from one another.

> **GRENZERFAHRUNG** • *Grenzerfahrung* is German and literally means "boundary experience," an experience that tests our abilities and ideas to the limit.

In summary, we can say that learning new concepts happens best when we become aware of their boundaries. In general language usage, this is designated "expanding one's horizons," or simply constantly trying out new things. If we push ourselves to the limit and make so-called *Grenzerfahrungen*, even negative experiences themselves can help us to define and perceive the positive more sharply. If we have never experienced failure, we do not know our own boundaries, which ultimately diminishes either our self-esteem or our well-being.

---

separate concepts.

[13] As the adjective reveals, the concept here would be "horse," and "blue" is simply the measurement of the color of the horse.

## 1.6.2.3  Concept Hierarchies

**Question**

How are contradictions in statements related to concepts?

First having found individual concepts, we can then use these concepts as the basis for new, specialized concepts. Hence, we need not consider each situation separately. If we apply these dependencies of specialized to more general concepts, a type of tree structure arises—a *concept hierarchy*. Each branch constitutes a general concept, and each leaf constitutes a more specialized concept.

The trunk (the "root") constitutes the most general ("entity") and a leaf a specialized concept (e.g., "softcover book") of the corresponding concept hierarchy (see Figure 1.6). In this model, a concept lying further out inherits the properties of the more general concept. For example, "table" is a specialization of "furniture." For this reason, the higher-level concept always encompasses ("inherits") all entities of the more specialized concept, while the specialized concept encompasses only a portion of the entities of the higher-level concept. This strict dependency and succession of the concepts are of great importance and a necessary prerequisite for our work with concepts.[14] The hierarchy permits us to learn many different concepts without having to re-comprehend and describe the world from the ground up each time.

---

[14] cf. Rand, Binswanger, and Peikoff, *Introduction to Objectivist Epistemology*, pp. 43,106.

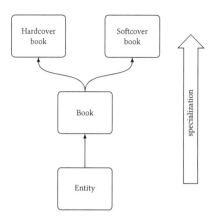

**Figure 1.6:** Example of the specialization of a general concept "entity" and "book" to "hardcover book" and "softcover book"

> **CONCEPT HIERARCHY** • A *concept hierarchy* is a tree-like structure consisting of concepts, defined by the definitions of given connections (e.g., "chair" and "table" are furniture, the concept "furniture" would thus constitute the root of a tree and "chair" and "table" are two successive branches).

> **INHERITANCE (OF A CONCEPT)** • A concept with an *inheritance of another concept* builds upon the other concept's definition. If the concept "table" inherits from the concept "matter," the former would build upon the property "mass" of the latter.

> **HIERARCHY TREE (OF CONCEPTS)** • A *hierarchy tree of concepts* refers to the directional ordering of concepts according to their inheritance.

In philosophy, this kind of structure of concepts is called the *genus proximum et differentia specifica* and traces its origins as far back as Aristotle. It consists of a *genus*—the overarching, more general concept—and a *differentia*—an attribute by means of which we can differentiate the concept from other concepts. In the case of "a female human," "female" (the gender) is the *differentia* ("female" categorizes humans into women and "non-women") and "human" is the *genus* (see Figure 1.7).

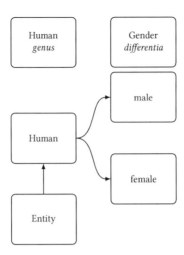

**Figure 1.7:** Difference between *genus* and *differentia*

To conclude, it should be noted that with the aid of theoretical knowledge about concepts, we can also examine our own concept hierarchy in our mind. This can be done by systematically considering each concept, level by level, and checking for contradictions. Should we stumble upon (apparent) contradictions in the course of using concepts, there must be either a classification of an entity under the wrong concept, or a faulty definition of that concept.

---

**Idea**

The origin of contradictions lies either in the faulty definition of concepts or in the faulty allocation of entities to concepts.

### 1.6.2.4 Conceptual Common Denominator

Sometimes it can indeed be practical to loosen this strictly tree-like structure a bit. To illustrate, the concept "mammal" applies to humans just as well as the concept "biped" does, although "mammal" and "biped" are almost independent concepts, coinciding only on a completely abstract level in the hierarchy tree (e.g., "bipeds" and "mammals" represent matter which moves by itself). We could now either define both concepts twice ("two-legged mammals", "four-legged mammals," "mammals," "bipeds," and "quadrupeds"), or we just define them individually and allow *combinations* of concepts. The first alternative is shown in Figure 1.8 on the left, the second one, with the so-called *conceptual common denominator*, on the right.

> **CONCEPTUAL COMMON DENOMINATOR** • If a concept inherits from more than one other concept, these additional concepts will be called *conceptual common denominators*. For example, we can classify a "human" entity into the concept "mammal" just as well as the concept "biped."

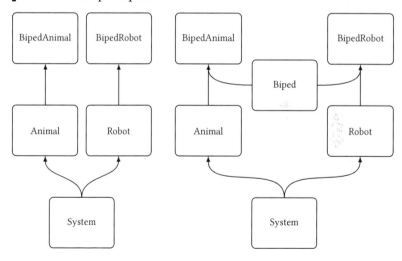

**Figure 1.8:** Example of a conceptual common denominator

The right-hand illustration in Figure 1.8 allows us to abstract a property already understood and use it again for a multitude of concepts. For instance, we can expect that a two-legged robot climbing stairs will have to overcome similar challenges as those faced by a human climbing stairs. Likewise, while sharks and dolphins are both sea animals, they merely represent very distant biological relatives. But owing to their similar living conditions, we will presumably find correspondingly similar properties in areas such as body shape, movement, or skin. A conceptual common denominator such as "sea organism" could thus help us better understand the world of sea animals, as we can re-apply insights about properties such as the streamlined body shape to a whole variety of animals without having to repeatedly examine each individually.

With conceptual common denominators, we must take care that there is no overlap of properties. An "ape-like horse" may ascribe typical character properties of an ape to a horse but, due to the multitude of overlapping properties between the concepts "horse" and "ape," this is difficult to determine solely by means of the expression.[15]

### 1.6.2.5  Boundary Cases

The opposite of the aforementioned *Grenzerfahrungen* are boundary cases, when we are not trying to explore the extremes of a concept, but instead cannot decide whether an entity belongs to one concept or another. To illustrate, imagine a line on the floor; we throw a number of dice into the vicinity of the line and establish two concepts: "left die" and "right die." As a definition, we stipulate that a die touching the line belongs to the side containing the larger part of it. With this setup—even with the best measuring techniques— undecidable cases can occur. Does this mean that our method of establishing the concept was faulty and that we need a third concept

---

[15]cf. Rand, Binswanger, and Peikoff, *Introduction to Objectivist Epistemology*, pp. 41–42.

for such a borderline case? Would there not also be a need for other borderline cases, thus leading to the collapse of our complete system of reasoning for concepts?

---

*Example*

In philosophy, this problem is known as "sorites," or the "sorites paradox": "When is a mound of sand a mound of sand?" or "How long does a mound of sand remain as such if we remove individual grains?"

With this, people try to suggest that we could not *really* perceive the world by means of concepts and that we would have to live always with a "fuzziness" in our knowledge.

---

But actually, there is an answer to this "paradox." It becomes clear if we step back for a moment and remember the definition of concepts. An essential part was the *omission* of measurements. So, whenever we can achieve the classification of an entity into a certain concept only through a measurement, we have to re-examine our concept hierarchy. We have to unify all concepts that are dependent on a certain measurement into an overriding concept. Next, for the definition of this new, more general, concept, we discard the measurement and replace it with a property.

The general idea is that we should proceed economically and keep the number of concepts as big as necessary but as small as possible. If we face concepts like "small table" and "large table" and have difficulties categorizing a "medium-sized table" in one of these concepts, we create a more general concept "table" and add the size of the table, as a property, to the definition. Simply put: a table is a table, whether it is located at the moment in a house or a garden, and whether it is blue or green, small or large.[16]

---

[16]cf. Rand, Binswanger, and Peikoff, *Introduction to Objectivist Epistemology*, pp. 101–4.

With the example of the dice and line, measurements are necessary, concepts of the type "left die" and "right die" thus cannot exist. Instead, a "die" would have a property "position," whose value we measure or set in relation to something else. In the example of the mound of sand, the error lies in a somewhat different place. If we answer the question about the mound of sand with "Define mound of sand!" then the dance around the question begins, since the questioner does not want to concede for the purposes of the argument that mounds of sand consist of a number of grains of sand, and single grains of sand also constitute a number. This behavior usually marks the point in our discussion at which the opposite side begins to cast doubt on the objectivity of language.

The origin of such imprecise concepts lies with Plato. He argued that there had to be a *third* truth value. Questions like: "What is the difference between an amount of sand and a mound of sand?", "How many grains of sand does it take to constitute a mound of sand?", or "Is a single grain of sand a mound of sand?" imply that there was a third logical condition besides "true" and "false," hence it is called the "argument of the law of excluded middle."

This type of argumentation is often used as an attack on concept formation. First, a concept is erroneously connected with a measurement ("Mounds of sand consist of at least three grains of sand"), then the absurdity of such a definition is pointed out, and finally it is declared that you cannot define concepts because of that. This ultimately leads to a situation where we no longer can make any clear statements about the world, particularly about truth values. This is a fallacy of the stolen concept. Whenever we encounter an argument like this, we should discuss the *underlying* concept and the incorporated measurements, and not be fooled into arguing about the *boundaries* of the imprecisely defined concept.

### 1.6.2.6 Concepts in Computers

I propose to consider the question, "Can machines think?"

—Alan Turing, *Computing Machinery and Intelligence*

---

**Question**

How do humans and computers compare in terms of comprehending an actual issue?

---

With a thorough, theoretical understanding of concepts, we can also easily pass on this structure of knowledge to other conscious entities. By this, we obviously mean first and foremost the consciousness of other *humans*, but we also see advances being made, especially in communication with other life forms. While we could never conceivably communicate with, for example, dolphins in the human sense, our knowledge of concepts can at least classify which stage of development other animals have reached in comparison to humans. Other than humans and animals, in the last century there has arisen a completely new domain of application: the computer.

A computer is something like an industrious worker who can take out, read, describe, and compare file cards from a large file catalog. Though it may require a great number of file cards, in principle, such a computer can solve any problem, be it coordinating a global network, deciphering the human genome, or designing a modern automobile. This basic model of a computer is called a "Turing machine," invented by Alan Turing in 1936.

Biography—**Alan Turing**

Alan Turing (1912 – 1954) was a British pioneering computer scientist, mathematician, logician, cryptanalyst and theoretical biologist. He was highly influential in the development of computer science. Turing is widely considered to be the father of theoretical computer science, artificial intelligence, and evolutionary computation. He is one of the many silent heroes that contributed to winning the Second World War against Nazi-Germany by cracking their "Enigma" code, an encryption protocol that was used for military communication. Tragically, after the war, he became a victim of prejudice against homosexuality.

Some readers might remember a time when searching for a book meant visiting an actual library, and opening an index-card cabinet with alphabetically sorted cards, one for each book. On each card, there was the book's full name, author, category, and location in the library. With that information, you could easily find the book in question on the shelves. You can imagine that each card is like an abstracted entity based on the definition of the concept of a book in a library. This kind of index system describes the situation of the available books in the library very well.

Actually, we can expand such an index-card system to describe *any* situation. We just need to add additional types of file cards and the possibility for a file card to reference another card. This is exactly what we have discussed earlier in terms of a concept hierarchy, definitions, and entities. The difference compared to a computer is that a computer processes those file cards digitally and much more quickly than a human can. Thus, a modern computer can "understand" any situation it is programmed to and "think" conceptually in a similar way as we do. To describe the concept hierarchy in a computer, we use so-called *object-oriented programming* languages.[17] With their aid, we can efficiently depict any real situation on a computer. By "efficiently," we mean that we can refer to existing parts of programs (existing concepts) in new situations—just as we ourselves use already known concepts to understand new situations.

> **Idea**
>
> A computer is like a large stack of indexed file cards in which a programmer can represent a concept hierarchy similar to our own in a structured way. Both computers and humans use concept hierarchies to categorize elements of a situation.

> **Did you know?**
>
> The knowledge behind concept hierarchies can be programmed into a computer with the help of a programmer. Programming a computer to create concepts *on its own* (using its sense data) is much more difficult, though. For this, we need an understanding of induction and deduction. With a better understanding of philosophy and human creativity, science is steadily making progress to create a computer program whose behavior resembles human intelligence. But will it also be self-aware?
>
> $\longrightarrow$ Read more in *Philosophy for Heroes: Continuum*

Let us consider this tangibly by reference to the example of a pizza delivery company. There, orders, inquiries, customers, and employees must be managed. The first step of management is an accurate grasp of the current situation. Instead of verbally surveying each

---

[17]Note that there was no direct connection between Objectivism and the emergence of object-oriented programming languages (cf. Reed, *Object-oriented programming and Objectivist epistemology: Parallels and implications*).

employee and customer and placing a summary in a file, we abstract
the properties of the relationship to each respective person. The employees may have much to tell about their lives, but only a few items
of data are important for the payment of their wages, such as a name
and bank account number. The same holds for the client, for whom
we actually require only a delivery address. In addition, we must
manage our products (the pizzas) and the individual inquiries and
orders. Just as in the construction of our concept hierarchy, here
also we try to determine the properties of an entity and disregard
all other information.

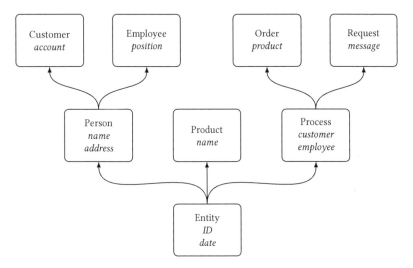

**Figure 1.9:** Concept hierarchy of a simplified description of a company

As all the parts of our company designated above should at the same
time refer to identifiable entities with a creation date, they should inherit from a more general concept named "entity." And obviously,
"clients" and "employees" are persons; we can thus let properties
such as the address inherit from a more general concept, "person."
With the definition of "order" and "request," we must in both cases
reference the person placing the order (*customer*) and the employee
processing the order (*employee*), and thus generalize the properties

in a concept called "process." Let us supplement these definitions with properties of the customer (his *account*), the employee (his *position* in the company), the order (the ordered *product*), and the request (the customer's *message*); we now obtain a schematic construction of this small slice of the world as in Figure 1.9.

*Example*

A further example for a common problem that we can solve with a computer with the help of concept hierarchies would be the ordering of a plane ticket. For each passenger, this proceeds according to a very similar model: the flight plan, flight conditions, seat assignment, and personal data, among other things, must be managed and monitored. Without these essential concepts, we would have to require every single passenger to write a summary of how she envisions her trip. Different people might like to spend the trip watching a movie, be served a hearty lunch on a short domestic flight, or postpone the flight by a half hour. Organizing a flight with more than one hundred people while observing all of these special, possibly conflicting, requests would be very time-consuming, if not impossible, without using a concept hierarchy.

### 1.6.3 Induction and Deduction

**Question**

How does the process of deduction supplement the process of induction?

Now we know how to design concepts and a concept hierarchy, and how to assign to the concepts corresponding definitions. We have also learned how we perceive reality and how we can protect ourselves from errors and external influences. So far, we have left open the question, how we can apply this knowledge, especially our concept hierarchy, in specific situations. In relation to this, philosophy discusses two concepts, *induction* and *deduction*:

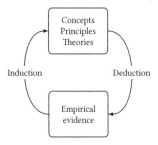

**Figure 1.10:** With induction, we reason from sense data (empirical evidence) the general case (concepts, principles, theories); with deduction, we learn more about an entity on the basis of our concepts (our knowledge).

**INDUCTION** • With *induction*, we conclude from the special case (a number of concrete perceptions) the general case (the concept). With this, we create new or refine existing concepts, on the basis of sense data and the logical integration of a number of perceptions of entities. For example, if we see a number of cars with different colors, we create from this observation the more general concept "car" by using induction.

**DEDUCTION** • With *deduction*, we conclude from the general case the special case. For this, we use the knowledge that we gained from induction, check if a certain perception fits the definition of a concept, and conclude for the corresponding entity that it has all the properties of the corresponding concept. In short, deduction is the process of subsuming new instances under a known concept (cf. Rand, Binswanger, and Peikoff, *Introduction to Objectivist Epistemology*, p. 28). Deduction thus operates in the opposite direction as induction. For example, if we notice that cars can drive on the street, and we see a parked car, then we can deduct that this car is able to drive on the street as well, because we have assigned the parked car to the known concept "car."

What we have discussed in the previous chapters relates to induction. We have made sense perceptions on the basis of sense data, integrated those, and finally created concepts. Figure 1.10 shows us the central element of the acquisition of new knowledge (induction) on one side, and the application of familiar knowledge (deduction) on the other. With induction, we conclude from the special case the general case. On the other hand, with deduction, we conclude from the general case the special case. For this, we use the knowledge that we gained from induction, check if a certain perception fits the definition of a concept, and conclude for the corresponding entity that it has all the properties of the corresponding concept.

## 1.6.4 Rationalism

> The earlier [concepts are] required to get to the later, but the later is required thoroughly to understand the earlier. So the only time you get a complete understanding of *any* element is when you know *every* element, and that is what it means to say it's a *system* of philosophy, an *integration*, and not simply a series of discrete items.

—Leonard Peikoff, *Understanding Objectivism*

The idea that knowledge can be obtained by the mere deduction from concepts that originate from one's mind or some place other than the external world is called *rationalism*. Is it possible to simply take our thoughts as a starting point and then reach conclusions about reality step by step, as rationalists like Descartes with his famous quote *"Cogito, ergo sum"*—*"I think, therefore I am"*—suggested?

**RATIONALISM** • *Rationalism* is the attempt to create knowledge without induction and to deduce from this knowledge.

**Question**

Are we spirits who discovered their bodies, or the other way around?

Naturally, it is true that if we think, we also exist. We do not, however, exist *because* we think. In order to *be aware* of something, we first must *exist* ourselves and *something* must exist we can be aware of; thus, something must exist in the first place. Our actual existence hence does not follow from simply being aware.[18]

---

[18] cf. Peikoff, *Objectivism: The Philosophy of Ayn Rand*, pp. 17–23.

In Objectivism, this statement is referred to as "primacy of existence" (as opposed to "primacy of *consciousness*"). We are aware of something because we exist. The entity of which we are to become aware must first exist before we can become aware of it. Our consciousness *observes* reality; it does not alter reality by our thoughts. Correspondingly, knowledge can be acquired only by directing our consciousness to reality using our senses. Likewise, as rationalism does not start with sense perceptions, one can usually find rationalists among those who doubt the validity of our senses.

Despite its name, the concept "primacy of existence" simply means that existence is *not* derived from consciousness. It does *not* mean that it stands in the first place or that you can derive the other axioms from it. Consequently, in Ayn Rand's argumentation, it never stands on its own and is instead used primarily as a counter-argument to the "primacy of consciousness" argument where people argue that things can come into existence via mere thought. A more fitting term would probably be "non-primacy of consciousness."

However, even if the result of an induction is drawn upon, but deduction is then used exclusively in the investigation of a certain fact, we can nonetheless still attribute it to rationalist thinking. Deduction is a very powerful tool, but the proper usage of logic does not happen automatically. As we will see in the following chapters and books, the risk of error is great if we cannot, or do not want to, check results from logic objectively each time by means of observations of reality.[19] So we see that induction and deduction ideally always go hand in hand.[20] We have to constantly go back and forth between the application of logic and the actual observation of reality.

---

[19]cf. Peikoff, *Understanding Objectivism*, pp. 209–41.
[20]cf. Rand, Binswanger, and Peikoff, *Introduction to Objectivist Epistemology*, pp. 94–111.

> **Idea**
>
> We are not spirits that deduce from their consciousness that
> they also must possess bodies. We are also not bodies who
> have learned to perceive the world and form a consciousness.
> We are both at the same time and we need to discover both
> at the same time.

### 1.6.5 Induction and Empiricism

In our discussion of cognition, the question still remained whether
induction is a valid process at all. Similar to what we have already
found, namely that ontology (the axioms) and epistemology are
closely intertwined, and similar to how we have to reflect on our
process of cognition, the process of induction is not structured in a
strictly hierarchical manner. The validity of induction depends on
the validity of induction itself, which leads to the so-called "problem of induction." Here, we want to examine this issue more closely
and examine the positions of various philosophers concerning *empiricism*. The discussion serves to provide different points of view
and the contradictions that lie in them in order to arrive at a clear
statement about how we can answer the question of validity of induction.

> **EMPIRICISM** • *Empiricism* states that the source of all knowledge
> lies in sense data (empirical evidence). In empiricism, deduction
> from knowledge which is not based on sense data is not possi-
> ble.

> **TABULA RASA** • *Tabula rasa* refers to the view that we are born
> without any innate knowledge and that our minds can create
> knowledge only with the help of sense data.

> **A PRIORI KNOWLEDGE** • *A priori knowledge* is knowledge that
> was acquired without first engaging in an experience.

Empiricism says that the source of all knowledge lies in sense data. This can go to the extreme by denying induction—for proving induction you first would need induction itself. At the same time, it is assumed that our mind is *tabula rasa* and contains no *a priori knowledge*, and therefore any knowledge can only be created with the help of sense data. Formulated this way, it would constitute a circular argument because you would have to have the knowledge about gaining knowledge before gaining knowledge in the first place. On the other hand, if we were to ignore sense data as the *only* source of knowledge and thus not apply induction, we would suddenly face a conundrum: how to prove without induction that an external reality exists at all.[21]

### 1.6.5.1 A World Without Induction

> **Question**
>
> How would the concept of "concept" lose its meaning in extreme empiricism?

Let us first take a look at a world without induction. Here, every situation would have to be considered anew, making the knowledge that we have so far acquired (using induction) useless. For an extreme empiricist, every realization is independent of the next, so everything is an independent, separate part of reality. Acquiring new knowledge would be a new challenge each time, since we could not build upon, or classify our observations into, already existing concepts. This extreme empirical mode of thought becomes particularly recognizable with the use of the so-called "cliff-jumper" argument.

---

[21]cf. Rand, *For the New Intellectual*, p. 173.

*Example*

The "Cliff-jumper" argument involves the notion that we can only judge something if we have experienced it ourselves. If that were the case, we would first have to jump from a particular cliff in order to be able to argue for or against jumping from that cliff. This view originates from extreme empiricism, according to which there are supposedly no general principles in nature, but only statements applicable to a given situation. For an extreme empiricist, each new jump from a cliff would always be a new unknown—we could not draw conclusions from past observations that we could apply to the future or other similar situations.

**Idea**

In extreme empiricism, the concept hierarchy tree would be completely flat and the concept of "concepts" would lose its meaning, because every concept would correspond only to one single instance.

## 1.6.5.2 The Problem of Induction

> The question of whether or not when you see something, you see only the light or you see the thing you're looking at, is one of those dopey philosophical things that an ordinary person has no difficulty with. Even the most profound philosopher, sitting eating his dinner, has many difficulties making out that what he looks at perhaps might only be the light from the steak, but it still implies the existence of the steak which he is able to lift by the fork to his mouth. The philosophers, who were unable to make that analysis, and that idea have fallen by the wayside from hunger.

—Richard Feynman, 1979, University of Auckland

**Question**

Can statements be shown to be true without induction? Why or why not?

In his *Critique of Pure Reason*, Kant wished to argue against the extreme empiricism of David Hume, and to overcome the antagonism between empiricism and rationalism. Hume claimed that induction in relation to causality could not be a means of learning anything about nature, since the justification of the validity of induction would, in turn, require induction. According to Hume, it is not valid to posit that the identity of an entity at a future point in time (without external influence and with attention paid to internal processes) is the same as in the present. This problem increases even further if we think about how this would mean that we could no longer rely on a constant structure of our sense organs and that we could perceive random disconnected static from the world.

Kant attempted to solve this problem by creating the term "synthetic *a priori* statement."[22] By that, he intended to show that there are statements about the world which would not require induction, meaning that certain truths about the world could be found without the need for sense data. His attempt failed, but it is helpful to understand his train of thought in that regard:

> **ANALYTIC STATEMENT** • An *analytic statement* is a statement whose assertion is given by the definition of the subject. As a result, measurements are not necessary to determine whether it is true or not (e.g., "Triangles have three vertices").

> **SYNTHETIC STATEMENT** • A *synthetic statement* is a statement whose assertion is given *not* by the definition of the subject alone; i.e., measurements are required to determine whether it is true or not (e.g., "*This* form has three corners").

> *A PRIORI* **STATEMENT** • An *a priori statement* is a statement that can be substantiated independently of experience (e.g., mathematical statements).

> *A POSTERIORI* **STATEMENT** • An *a posteriori statement* is a statement that must be substantiated through experience (for example, "bodies are heavy;" we must first lift a body to determine its weight).

In his work, Kant sought *synthetic statements* which were at the same time *a priori statements* and, as a result, could be substantiated without sense data (empirical knowledge) of reality. His lengthy explanation in his *Critique of Pure Reason* did not help to clarify what he—knowingly or unknowingly—actually meant by his notion of analytic and synthetic statements, as well as by the distinction of *a priori* and *a posteriori statements*.

The point is that his synthetic statements concern nothing other than *measurements*. A *synthetic* statement is thus nothing other

---

[22] cf. Kant, *Critique of Pure Reason*, pp. 43–56.

than a statement about the *effect* of a representation of a concept —an entity. The statement "All chairs are made of material" refers to a *property* of the concept "chair,"while the statement "All chairs are made of the material wood" relates to the *tangible effect* of the property "material." A synthetic *a priori* statement thus would be nothing other than a statement whose assertion is not given by the definition of the subject (*i.e., a measurement!*), but can be substantiated independently of experience (*i.e., not a measurement!*). A measurement that is not a measurement is obviously a contradiction; for this reason, by the Axiom of Identity, synthetic *a priori* statements cannot exist. Thus, his "solution" is not a solution and the problem persists.

---

**Idea**

By the Axiom of Identity, Kant's synthetic *a priori* statements cannot exist. That means that there are no statements that can be shown to be true without induction. Kant's examination does not solve the problem of induction.

---

**Question**

What does Hume's problem of induction have to do with omniscience?

---

If a question seems unsolvable, the question itself should be inspected more closely. In regard to induction, Hume concerns himself with the future, and hence with the question of whether knowledge we acquire about the world can be applied to future events. "Time," however, is ultimately merely a construct of the mind. In more general terms, it deals with the question of whether knowledge acquired from a past situation is also valid in a situation at different points in time. Still more generally, his position could be seen as a criticism of the use of concepts.

If we have established that when dropping a certain apple, it falls downward, who is to say that the same must also hold for a different apple (or at a different but comparable location or point in time)? Possible answers to this problem include that we may have erred in constructing the concepts in question, and there are still many more significant properties we might have not yet discovered. But that is not what Hume aims at; he is concerned about the validity of concepts, whether we can acquire general knowledge about the world when we *exclude such special cases.* We have defined "concept" in this way for the very reason that it includes entities that, for example, possess the property of falling downward. It makes no difference whether we now consider other apples in our fruit basket or apples existing far in the future. In both cases, we are referring to the same concept, "apple." If future apples possess other properties than our present apples, we just have to diversify our concept "apple." When defining the concept, we have to either restrict the selection of entities or include a dynamic component which adds the factor of time into the description of the properties.

Exactly such a discussion is currently going on in the sciences concerning the gravitational constant. If, for instance, in the future, the gravitational constant should change, it would say nothing about the validity of concepts *per se* but instead would speak to our potentially incomplete definition of gravitation, where we should have included a change of the gravitational constant depending on the time and location. Hume himself stated the example that we could not know that the sun would continue to rise in the East just because we have observed so in the past. But the point is that we can expand our concept and knowledge about the stars and planets to include irregularities without having to declare them as special cases (think of a morning solar eclipse).

Ultimately, we see that Hume's argument is a matter of nonexistent omniscience in the formation of concepts. We can, therefore, compare it with Kant's "things in themselves": potentially, there is always a level further on, an unknown "true reality," which was as yet unknown to us when we defined our concepts. We could also formulate the question in more general terms: does *carrying out* a deduction depend on sense data (empirical evidence)? Can we perform experiments which can determine whether we can determine things? This approach leads to an endless cycle of questioning—to answer the question we must first be able to answer the question. It has come to this recursion, since we cannot ask a question which attacks the very presupposition for the question itself—this would be a fallacy of the stolen concept. We could not then bring into question the validity of concepts if we pose a question that uses concepts.

> **Idea**
>
> Hume's problem of induction is ultimately directed at the fact that we are not omniscient when we establish concepts.

### 1.6.5.3 The Truth

People say to me, "Are you looking for the ultimate laws of physics?" No, I'm not, I'm just looking to find out more about the world and if it turns out there is a simple ultimate law that explains everything, so be it, that would be very nice to discover. If it turns out it's like an onion with millions of layers and we're just sick and tired of looking at the layers, then that's the way it is! But whatever way it comes out, it's nature, it's there, and she's going to come out the way she is. And therefore, when we go to investigate, we shouldn't pre-decide what it is we are trying to do except to find out more about it.

—Richard Feynman, *The Pleasure of Finding Things Out*

One answer to the problem of induction is that knowledge is more than just an accumulation of instances. If we relied only on induction, our (inductive) claims of the world would be invalidated regularly by new discoveries and we would have to start again and again from scratch. Inductive claims are disconnected, they rely on a "traditionalist" view where the future will resemble the past. What we need to do is *connect* our knowledge, *integrate* it into a whole. When creating the concept of a swan, we should keep in mind that we might find outliers and irregularities, especially if we have no idea yet about how a swan becomes a swan (by biology, genetics, etc.). The same applies to the rising sun in the morning. After we gained knowledge about planetary movements, our inductive claim became an *objective* one because we could explain it not just with past data, but also with the principles that govern past data. And when we refined our knowledge later with the theory of relativity, it did not invalidate the principles we came up with before, as it was a more accurate description of reality.

Of course, this approach does not solve the problem of induction itself. And none of the so-called great philosophers like Descartes, Hume, or Kant were able to provide a solution for the problem of induction. And what we have seen is that there is no solution to it! It is a pseudo-problem which we actually should not use, especially not if it puts our ability to understand the world into question. Just because we can ask the question does not mean that there is a solution. Or that if we do not find a solution, there is something wrong with our perception of the world. The point is that the problem of induction is an impossible question whose only real answer is *omniscience*. So, at most, what we owe to Hume and others is that we should not assume that we are omniscient; we should require proof for scientific theories and re-examine existing knowledge when new insights are gained.

> **Did you know?**
>
> As we are looking only at a part of the universe, our "truths" include the context in which we have found them. As one truth builds on many others, we have to guard carefully everything that we have discovered. Our tool for that will be the *scientific method.*
>
> ⟶ Read more in *Philosophy for Heroes: Continuum*

In the end, the question is what we want. Do we want the "absolute truth"? Should the goal be to attain all knowledge and create an exact replica of the universe in our minds? Already, there is a device in the world that can make 100% accurate predictions of the future. It's called: the universe. It takes one second to calculate what it will look like in the next second. It uses all of its calculation power, all the atoms and molecules working together, creating a super computer which is faster and more accurate than anything built within that universe. We cannot compress the universe into our brains; we can perceive only one part of the universe at a time with our senses.

What we, as humans, *can* do is *filter* and *abstract* (concepts!) the information and focus only on parts of the universe at a time. We have to understand the principles of the known universe while hoping that the unknown parts will not interfere with our thinking. But because we are not omniscient, we cannot be sure and we have to expand our horizon constantly. We cannot take one piece of "absolute truth," close our senses, and then deduct everything from that piece of information without ever checking with reality. Basically, this is what the rationalistic fallacy is about, and that is also the reason our axioms, if they stand independently from epistemology, are not "absolute truths." We cannot say, "This is it, I have found the truth, I will ignore any new perceptions." We have to go back and forth between induction and deduction and refine our understanding (our concepts) of the world.

> Suppose that physics, or rather nature, is considered analogous to a great chess game with millions of pieces in it, and we are trying to discover the laws by which the pieces move. The great gods who play this chess play it very rapidly, and it is hard to watch and difficult to see. However, we are catching on to some of the rules, and there are some rules which we can work out which do not require that we watch every move. [...] We do not need to watch the insides to know at least something about the game.

—Richard Feynman, *Character of Physical Law*

Is it an unsatisfying answer that the universe does not consist of a set of independently perceivable truths? Well, nature does not care about whether she can be satisfyingly understood. We have to work with what we have. And what we do want, or should want, is a matter of ethics. Epistemology can only provide you with the means. Still, the question of what *we* want already implies that we have an identity. And philosophy teaches us to act in this world. Philosophy is not about discovering—as Kant put it—the "true reality." Maybe we do not know everything, and if we knew more, something else would follow. But based on what we have, we can make statements. They might ultimately turn out to be inaccurate because we did not include all the data, but we did the best we could, and we built upon our knowledge. The alternative would be to make no predictions at all, and wait forever until we have gathered so much data that we are omniscient. Likewise, we need to welcome new and reflect on old ideas; this is what opens our soul to discovering reality. The challenge is striking the right balance between reflection and action. This is the first building block on your path from a student of philosophy to a teacher and ultimately a leader.

# Chapter 2

# Language

 You can know the name of a bird in all the languages of the world, but when you're finished, you'll know absolutely nothing whatever about the bird [...] So let's look at the bird and see what it's doing—that's what counts. I learned very early the difference between knowing the name of something and knowing something.

—Richard Feynman, *What Do You Care What Other People Think? Further Adventures of a Curious Character*

In the first chapter we learned that philosophy relies on observation of reality. It is tempting to deduct philosophical answers from the examination of thoughts or language alone (rationalism). After all, with language, we can pose any question imaginable and thus give it a significant, but possibly undeserved, weight. But for the very reason we should *not* include linguistic examination, we need to examine what language is and the role it plays in our thoughts in order *not* to be tempted to use linguistics as a philosophical argument.

Often, philosophical questions stem from linguistic fallacies in the form of special sentence constructions, rhetorical questions, or ambiguous word usage. The prevention of this kind of rationalism will be the focus of this chapter. We will examine the origins of our languages and define the concept of language by examining differences among languages. Next, we will focus on the special case of the language of mathematics, and investigate to what extent it has a connection to reality, and which possible philosophical objections arise from mathematics, such as questions about infinity, irrational numbers, nothingness, or the universe. It is crucial to understand the basics of mathematics because, in philosophy, one is faced with mathematical arguments, for example with questions surrounding the concept of infinity. That is *rationalism* and refers to the attempt to deduce truths about the world without using empirical evidence.

In addition, so far we have taken for granted that we can communicate with each other *objectively*, i.e., that you can understand the meaning of the words I am using. That, of course, does not have to be the case. Just imagine if you had bought this book in a language unknown to you. No matter how thorough my explanations are, you would not understand anything. Thus, we have to clarify whether objective communication is possible at all, or if we can provide each other merely with random mental stimuli and are doomed to live in our own subjective world of thoughts. While we might find an objective language for our own thoughts, we might face conversation partners with different concept hierarchies, or definitions which might lead to misunderstandings or even a complete impossibility of communication.

## 2.1 Properties of Language

Our PERCEPTION OF THE WORLD began with the perception of entities and the consciousness of our own existence. From these first perceptions, we have formed an *entity-based language.* In contrast to this, *process-based language* is centered on representations of *changes* in entities *over time* (e.g., "it is raining," or "evolution"). Our language is a mixture of both entity-based as well as process-based language. Here, we discuss the simpler case of the description and communication of entities and their properties. This depicts the essence of our language: "What entities are there and what are their properties?"

---

**Did you know?**

Eastern philosophies focus much less on perceiving the world in terms of entities than Western philosophies do. Instead, they see the world and its parts as processes, with the entities (including humans) being just their temporary representatives.

⟶ Read more in *Philosophy for Heroes: Continuum*

---

The first form of language is a type of inner dialog. We all learned a certain connection while being fed as babies, namely that the consumption of food quells our (negative) feeling of hunger. This chain of thought occurs implicitly, without the aid of conventional spoken language; it simply takes place within us. The physical realization of this "language" is located only in our neuronal structures. It merely places certain sense perceptions in relation to one another and reinforces the connection between different experiences through repetition. We can also consciously refer back to this concept by remembering the respective concrete situation, thus placing into memory an image of our sense data of the moment, and contemplating it with our "mind's eye."

The concept of language—like any other concept—becomes clear only when we have become familiar with several different languages. We have to get to know the limits of a concept in order to be able to define it clearly. Our use of the term *language* is far broader than merely referring to specific languages such as German, English, or Spanish. There are many different languages whose elements arose coincidentally or out of convenience, while other elements represent essential components. These languages differ in complexity, expressive power, degree of completeness, degree of precision, and translatability. We can communicate with sounds, music, hand signals, writing, or merely with our eyes.

Language is ultimately the *physical realization*, i.e., the application of concepts: each instance of the creation and use of concepts involves a form of language. The degree of complexity with which this language can be constructed can be limited by our *physical* capabilities. But as soon as we can contemplate a certain number of concepts, whether simultaneously or in sequence, all the possibilities are open to us and we can—step by step—construct an indefinitely large concept hierarchy tree.

In addition, in most cases, language consists of units which are sharply delimited from one another. A word should not relate to a different concept because of small changes in the pronunciation. This plainly stems from the "noise" in everyday speech: communication would be difficult if, for example, the word "mouse" spoken more loudly corresponded to "elephant." Likewise, there would be problems in written correspondence due to different fonts or hand-writing: just because you write a word in bold, its concept does not change. There are, in fact, such cases in our own language, namely homonyms, whose pronunciation determines their meaning (homo-graphs, "bear" as in "animal" vs. "bear" as in "to support or carry"), or whose meaning is different but whose pronunciation is the same (ho-mophones, "rose" as in "plant" vs. "rose" as in "past tense of rise"). The advantage of a language with sharply delimited units also be-comes apparent with *whistled* languages which you can encounter mostly in mountainous regions, in dense forests, in regions with spread-out settlements, or in connection with hermetic professions like shepherding. The volume differences that are required to trans-port a message over longer distances do not have any effect on the conceptual contents of the message. A similar concept can be found in our telephone system: analog transmission of sound (the sound waves you speak into the telephone) was replaced by digital trans-mission of sound: first, your sound waves are encoded into 0s and 1s, transmitted to the receiver, and then again decoded into sound waves.

We can also use gestures complementary to spoken language. "[T]hey provide information that cannot be derived from the spo-ken utterance alone [...] information about the speed and direction of movement, about the relative position of people and objects, and about relative size of people and objects."[1] At the same time, our bodies outwardly express an uninterrupted, passive communication. Each movement can be interpreted and thus gives some indication of our frame of mind. To conclude, gestures refer to *measurements*. Given the medium at hand, we will focus on written language in the further course of this chapter, and only occasionally refer to gestures like pointing at things. Let us first take a look at the concepts:

---

[1] Mithen, *The Singing Neanderthals—the Origins of Music, Language, Mind, and Body*, pp. 155–56.

**SITUATION** • A *situation* consists of a certain number of entities, their changes in properties, their mutual interactions, and their relationships to one another, at certain times and in certain places.

**IMAGE** • An *image* is an entity that is linked to another entity by a mental connection.

**LANGUAGE** • A *language* is a system by means of which we can translate knowledge of a situation (and concepts) into a series of images and supporting linguistic constructs, and conversely, translate a series of images and linguistic auxiliary constructs into knowledge of a situation (and concepts). Language is the application of concepts and the hierarchy of these concepts.

The aforementioned *images* take shape in written language as follows:

**LETTER** • A *letter* is a small symbol or image ("a," "b," "c," etc.).

**WORD** • A *word* consists of a number of ordered letters.

**SENTENCE** • A *sentence* consists of a number of ordered words.

**NOUN** • A *noun* is a word that stands as a representative of an entity (proper noun, e.g., "Peter") or a concept (common noun, e.g., "dog").

**VERB** • A *verb* is a word that refers to the changes in properties of a noun (e.g., an action: "Peter *runs*").

**ADJECTIVE** • An *adjective* is a word that describes a corresponding noun in more detail. It adds a measurement to a property of the corresponding concept (e.g., "a *tall* tree").

**ADVERB** • An *adverb* is a word that refers to a verb and compares the mode or degree of change in properties with another change in properties (e.g., "She treaded down the hallway *quietly*"); alternatively, an adverb can relate to an adjective or another adverb and describe it more accurately (e.g., "He had *very* big eyes").

**SUBJECT** • A *subject* is the noun to which the verb refers as an origin (e.g., "*Peter* runs").

**OBJECT** • An *object* is a noun to which the verb refers as a target (e.g., "Peter throws the *ball*.").

We will now consider the question of the origin of writing, in order to have a framework in which to classify our modern language.

## 2.1.1 The Origin of Writing

In contrast to spoken language, we can trace the origin and development of writing through pieces of text recovered from antiquity. The central point of the development of language was the Ice Age, which ended approximately 12,000 years ago, when the temperature worldwide was as low as 10°C below the present average. As there was no knowledge of building or construction, humans sought refuge in caves, which, together with fire, offered protection from the elements, particularly wind. There arose the precursor of writing, in the form of cave paintings, through which a tribe was able to relate its history and preserve its culture (and hence its social cohesion, which proved important to survival). Tribe members could pass on important knowledge to the next generation, such as which parts of the body of an animal are vulnerable to attack, animal herd formations, or hunting strategies. Thus, whoever could interpret the drawings of their ancestors was a valuable member of the tribe. In addition, shamans who experienced hallucinations through trance, drug consumption, or oxygen deprivation in cave systems deep in the Earth were able to make those "visions" visible to others. During cave explorations, scientists have found the now-silent remains of these experiences. Deeply hidden in the underground, they have encountered symbols and pictures, including spirals, lines, and dots, dating back 100,000 years.[2]

---

[2]cf. Human Knowledge, *The Human Journey*.

Before reaching its present form, writing passed through a number of stages of development. A notable precursor took the form of transportable, inscribable objects which were used as a kind of signature or document for the exchange of goods. A 60,000-year-old example was unearthed in modern South Africa, showing repeating symbols inscribed on eggshells, which was at the time the oldest discovered artifact resembling writing.[3] According to theory, they served social interactions among the group.[4] These interactions became more and more important as increasing numbers of people assembled in one place. Whether as a protection against theft, due to a hierarchical societal structure, or simply for reasons of efficiency, food was stored centrally in temples or granaries and exchanged for inscribed clay tablets as an indication of ownership, similar to a currency.

Rooted in these cave paintings and tablet inscriptions, forms of writing gradually developed which depicted living conditions—at first concretely and then, over time, ever more abstractly, favoring simpler, more compact, and more meaningful linguistic representation. For a monolingual society, this proved to be the natural development, as all speakers shared the knowledge of how to correctly express chosen words upon recognizing them in writing. But this symbolic script turned out to be counterproductive, since people not only had to learn the spoken language itself, but also its independent, symbolic representation.

---

[3] cf. Bower, *Stone Age Engravings Found on Ostrich Shells.*

[4] cf. Texier et al., *A Howiesons Poort tradition of engraving ostrich eggshell containers dated to 60,000 years ago at Diepkloof Rock Shelter, South Africa.*

The Egyptian hieroglyphs developed in a society which saw itself as the center of the world—albeit understandably, in view of the technological, medical, and societal-organizational preeminence at the zenith of the Egyptian empire. They had little interest in maintaining relations with other peoples, and the strictly hierarchically organized society contributed little to widespread literacy. Writing was mostly reserved for specialists working in the service of the state. For them, the effort required to learn 1,000 to 5,000 different hieroglyphs was acceptable.[5]

**Question**

How did ancient sea-trading affect the development of our current alphabet?

A very different scene unfolded with the ascent of the ancient Phoenician civilization in about 1050 BC. Its means of existence consisted of widespread trading activity in the entire Mediterranean region. The Phoenicians undertook long trading journeys which brought them into contact with many different societies. In view of this, they required two things in terms of writing: widespread literacy in their own population, enabling them to secure investments and payment contracts, and a writing system that would be easy for their foreign trading partners to learn and translate. At the same time, this writing system would also be used to write down the *foreign* languages of those trading partners. Their solution was the use of a *phonetic alphabet*.

It was presumably this economic motivation that superseded the intuitive attempt to use pictures for terms in writing (such as the Egyptian hieroglyphs), in favor of the invention of the Phoenician alphabet. Thus, at the heart of written language, images of culturally pre-existing central motifs of daily life were replaced by a sys-

---

[5]Holst, *Phoenician Secrets—Exploring the Ancient Mediterranean*, pp. 227–30.

tem based on abstraction, which built upon the great commonality of all people: the *spoken* language.

> **PHONEME** • A *phoneme* is a sound syllable that represents a single unit of sound that a person can make. In the English language, there are about 44 phonemes.

If each *phoneme* is assigned a symbol, any given spoken language can be written down and read aloud, and the pronunciation can be learned along with the script. Over time, the Egyptians themselves moved progressively further from a picture-based representation toward the use of hieroglyphs as symbols for spoken syllables; but the societal and economic pressure on the development of writing was quite different than in the case of the Phoenicians.

---

### Example

A similar example to Egypt and Phoenicia would be China and Japan. In Japan, the *Kana* system, an alphabet with one symbol for each sound syllable, was invented in the 9th century while Chinese itself largely remained ideographic. Only recently (20th century), China adopted the *Pinyin* ("spelled sounds") system, allowing standardized transcription of Chinese based on sounds.

---

### Idea

Our present-day writing system descends from the Phoenician alphabet. It was a writing system that emerged in the ancient Mediterranean sea-trading environment and that depicted sounds used in speech (phonemes) instead of pictorial representations of concepts.

Due to its great economic significance, the Phoenician alphabet spread throughout the Mediterranean region. Without the alphabet (and the papyrus invented by the Egyptians and traded by the Phoenicians), there likely never would have been an *Iliad* or *Odyssey* in Greece by Homer, nor would the Roman Empire have taken over the Italian peninsula. It eventually developed, through a number of intermediate forms (Aramaic, Greek, Punic, ancient Hebrew, Etruscan, etc.), into the various present-day alphabets (Latin, Cyrillic, Hebrew, Arabic, etc.). This close relationship becomes clear when comparing the development of the alphabets:

- The Phoenician alphabetic script, 1000 BC.

  𐤀𐤁𐤂𐤃𐤄𐤅𐤆𐤇𐤈𐤉𐤊𐤋𐤌𐤍𐤎𐤏𐤐𐤑𐤒𐤓𐤔𐤕

- The Etruscan (predecessors of the Romans in Italy) alphabet, eighth century BC.

  ABΓDEFI⊟⊗IKL⋏⋎⊟OГM𐌓⋏ꟊTYX𐌘Y8

- The Greek alphabet, sixth century BC.

  ΑΒΓΔΕΖΗΘΙΚΛΜΝΞΟΠΡϺΤΥΧΦΨΩ

- The Old Latin alphabet, retaining B, D, K, O, Q, X but dropping Θ, Ś, Φ, Ψ, and F.

  ABCDEFZHIKLMNOPQRSTVX

Biography—**Homer**

Even in antiquity, Homer was a legend. He was so famous that it is not clear where, when, and if he lived at all or if he is used to represent a number of authors. He is assumed to be the author of the *Iliad* and the *Odyssey* and to have lived around 800 BC in ancient Greece. Both works count as some of the oldest extant works of Western literature. The stories are about the Trojan War (probably 1200 BC at the west coast of today's Turkey) and its aftermath. They tell us about protagonists and their individual struggles. They transcend the mere portrayal of inherently good or bad persons. Characters from gods to goatherd all show different right or erroneous thinking independent of their status. Still, Homer's world remains a supernatural one where events are explained with the personal will of the gods and not with causality. It was a world where gods are worshiped because they were powerful, not because they were moral.

**Did you know?**

The word "Bible," which literally means "the book," is derived from the name of the former Phoenician city of Byblos (Lebanon). It is the oldest continously inhabitated city of the world and was a central trading place for papyrus, the predecessor of paper. Likewise, the word "phonetic" (phonetic alphabet) is derived from "Phoenician."

$\longrightarrow$ Read more in *Philosophy for Heroes: Epos*

Now that we have classified our language *historically*, we will consider what types of language there are in terms of their expressibility.

## 2.1.2  Completeness and Consistency

> Poor creatures. Why must we destroy you? I'll tell you why.
> Order is the tide of creation, but yours is a species that wor-
> ships the one over the many. You glorify your intelligence
> because it allows you to believe... anything. That you have a
> destiny. That you have a right. That you have a cause. That
> you are special. That you are great. But in truth, you are born
> insane. And such misery, cannot be allowed to spread.

*—Starship Troopers 2: Hero of the Federation*

---

**Question**

What is an example of a consistent language? What is an
example of a complete one?

---

The movie *Starship Troopers 2: Hero of the Federation* is about an alien
insectoid race which criticizes the thought pattern of humankind
that allows humans to think and act independently of reality. It
takes this unpredictability as a reason to wage war against humanity. This criticism is somewhat justified as many of our conflicts
ultimately can be traced back either to fear of the unknown or to an
inconsistent use of language. While we can express everything with
our language ("complete"), it can be applied inconsistently because
of logical errors in our statements. The problem is that many ignore
this fact and assume that anything that can be said or asked using
language is worth examining. In the further progress of this book series, we will learn to identify invalid questions and to communicate
with others objectively.

Language constitutes a formal system which determines how we
have to combine words to form a statement. This system, however,

only provides formal rules, like a sentence must contain a subject and verb. But just because a sentence is formally correct concerning its spelling and grammar, this does not mean that the underlying *statement* of the sentence is connected to reality. You could ask "Why is it raining today?" when there was no rain that day at all. The question is grammatically correct yet makes no sense.

Specifically regarding the expressive ability of such formal systems like languages, we consider Gödel's *First Incompleteness Theorem*, proven by logician Kurt Gödel, to which we will frequently refer in the following discussion. The theorem states: *Each sufficiently powerful formal system is either inconsistent or incomplete.* It means that, if we use a language with which we can make statements ("sufficiently powerful"), it is either complete but inconsistent or incomplete but consistent.

**Idea**

Each (sufficiently powerful) formal system is either inconsistent or incomplete (Gödel's First Incompleteness Theorem).

### 2.1.2.1 Incomplete Languages

We know that we can use our language inconsistently because its grammar allows us to make statements like, "This statement is wrong." What would a consistent (but incomplete) language look like? Such a language assigns each situation a unique phoneme and contains no self-referential statements or combinable component parts (like subject, verb, object, etc.). Due to the finite number of phonemes, such a language is usable only on a very limited basis. We can imagine a basket of apples. For every new apple we put into the basket and for each other basket we encounter, we would have to invent a new phoneme.

Somewhat more complex languages at least permit the compounding of phonemes into words. A word is thus a specified unit in a vocabulary. But as with the phonemes, we would have to remember a unique word for each situation and for each combination of details.[6] The resulting virtually infinite number of expressions required to describe all situations makes this limited form of a language impractical. Consider that the description of all possible chess game positions would already require approximately $10^{50}$ (i.e., a 1 with 50 zeroes) different terms.[7]

However, despite its impracticality, this form of language remains, to a certain degree, an essential component of our linguistic culture. To illustrate, we could show a video from a vacation trip. In the absence of tampering, the video in itself would be free of contradictions since it simply reflects the light captured at certain time periods. But if we allow for editing, we would be once again in the realm of a complete but possibly inconsistent language. We could mix up the sequence of events, first showing ourselves on the mountaintop and only then during the climb up instead of the other way around. Even closer to reality than a video would be simply *pointing* to situations in our surroundings—the proto-language we always readily refer back to when we, or our counterpart, cannot speak the language of the country.

This leads us to the Pirahã, a small tribe of hunters and gatherers in the Amazon region whose language is clearly different from others in significant ways, as it is missing *self-reference*. Instead, each situation is described in separate sentences.[8] Their language comes relatively close to an "ideal" consistent language. For cultural reasons the Pirahã only express what is directly obvious; in their language, the ability to make self-referential statements is thereby limited, and

---

[6] cf. Zimmer, *So kommt der Mensch zur Sprache*, p. 22.

[7] As a comparison, the mass of the known universe is about $10^{50}$ tons.

[8] cf. Everett, *Das glücklichste Volk—Sieben Jahre bei den Pirahã-Indianern am Amazonas*, pp. 343–50.

thus we could even label them model empiricists. For instance, "My brother's house" would have to be expressed in separate sentences as "I have a brother. The brother has a house."

> What makes us human, that's what this debate is all about. Where does our language come from? Is our language some mysterious gene that somehow crept in our evolution? If so, that's worth knowing, that's very interesting. What I'm claiming is that culture can affect not just the words of a language but the entire grammar of a language. And I'm saying that the Pirahã are one clear example of this happening.
>
> —Daniel Everett, *The Grammar of Happiness*

This contradicts theories of an innate universal grammar proposed by linguists such as Noam Chomsky who considered self-reference as essential to all human grammar. Language structures are thus a product of our upbringing and culture—and language itself thereby represents a cultural artifact, a sort of technology, which has developed from generation to generation in our minds, but not in our genes.

Biography—**Daniel Everett**

Daniel Everett was born in 1951 in the United States and studied linguistics as part of the preparation for his work as a missionary in the Amazonian jungle. His main focus is the language of the Pirahã and how it related to Noam Chomsky's idea of universal grammar. During his expedition in the Amazonian jungle in the 1980s, he was confronted with the views of the Pirahã, which are very much rooted in reality. His failed attempts to convert them to Christianity ultimately lead to him becoming an atheist and positioning himself against one of the figureheads of linguistics, Chomsky. This courage to question what he thought was wrong is one of the traits of a hero. His book *Don't Sleep, There Are Snakes* renewed the academic discussion about whether recursivity is part of an inborn language ability of humans or not.

We can take a further example of a language related to reality from the Australian Aboriginal language *Guugu Yimithirr*. This language employs no self-referential terms when dealing with relations between objects in terms of their geographical location, and so there are no words for "left," "right," "in front," and "behind." Instead, the cardinal directions are used for this purpose. Thus, we would not ask whether someone could please move a little bit to the right, but whether he could move a little bit to the north.[9]

At first glance, this does not quite fit with the distinction between complete and consistent languages, i.e., it would violate Gödel's Incompleteness Theorem. With the knowledge of the cardinal directions, every statement would be true and consistent—and exact and impossible to misunderstand at that. Under closer investigation, however, the question arises of how the system could function *outside* its natural frame of reference (the Australian desert). In many lo-

---

[9]cf. Deutscher, *Does Your Language Shape How You Think?*

cations, such as underground, at the north or south poles, in Earth's orbit, on the moon, etc., we would have to establish a new frame of reference—here again a case of a consistent but *incomplete* language. Perfect for the desert where there are no significant landmarks, unusable for the application within a city.

### 2.1.2.2 Inconsistent Languages

The most widely spoken languages (such as Chinese, English, Spanish, and German) are instead *mixtures* of elements of both types of language and allow for *syntax*. Whenever we can choose from a limited number of alternatives in order to provide an exact representation of a situation, we prefer the consistent, rather than the complete, form of language.

> **SYNTAX** • In languages with *syntax*, words can be combined into sentences that each correspond to a meaning.

It should be emphasized, though, that the inconsistency of our complete language does not mean that we cannot practice philosophy, or that no statements at all can be true. Simply because we *can* form inconsistent statements, does not mean that *all* statements are affected. We should simply be *aware* of the limitations of language and realize that statements in themselves also can be contradictory, and that not every question must have an answer. If we refer to the statement within the very statement itself, we must exercise particular caution; we can think of a statement such as, "This statement is false."

*Example*

Think of a coffee vending machine. It is assumed by the producer that only certain types of coffee will be desired. For the customer, it often suffices to choose between those pre-defined programs like coffee or espresso. The machine presumably could brew many other variations of our desired beverage, with different brewing times or different concentrations of coffee. But we do without this multitude of possibilities, in favor of a defined program which is relatively foolproof and can be served simply and quickly. So in this case we prefer a consistent language over a complete one. When a machine offers too many options, it shows that the manufacturer did not know what the customer would expect from the machine, and the likelihood of maloperation increases.

Last but not least, the argument from Chapter 1.5, "Ontology," takes hold again. If through our language we could not describe a philosophy related to reality, by means of which we can make statements about reality, then we could especially make no statements about the language and its supposedly false depiction of reality. Every argument against the possibility of using language as an objective means of expression of philosophical statements would thus be an argument containing a stolen concept and thus would be contradictory.

We should always maintain a connection to reality, keep our definitions in mind and, through logic, try to attribute statements to reality, i.e., actual perceptions. This is at its root nothing else than the attempt to translate a statement of an inconsistent and complete language into a consistent but incomplete language—one connected to reality. Usually, this can be achieved by replacing terms with their definitions and by applying logic until the terms fit or conflict with perceptions of reality. "This is a tree" becomes "This is a plant with a trunk and branches with leaves." If we point (a consistent but incomplete language!) to a shrub, there is a contradiction and the statement would be wrong.

Obviously, this approach is of little practical use in daily life. If we applied it to every sentence, this would put a halt to most of our communication. On the other hand, in our daily use, we rely on someone else having done this kind of work for us—*the wise men and women of our human history*. With language, we learn not only vocabulary, but also the knowledge that underlies concepts and definitions. This kind of truth-seeking or linguistic examination becomes relevant when there are two different opinions about an issue. To solve this conflict, both sides have to climb down the concept hierarchy together. We have to ask for the definitions of the concepts we are using, and then continue until we find common ground. For example, we might differ in our definition of "democracy," but through this process, we might find that we agree on concepts like epistemology. Then we could discuss our *actual* fundamental differences and have a productive conversation.

### 2.1.3 Language Optimization

Languages differ not so much as to what can be said in them, but rather as to what it is relatively easy to say.

—Charles F. Hockett, *Chinese versus English: An exploration of the Whorfian theses*

**Question**

Aside from concept hierarchy, what makes languages complex?

Besides the distinction between completeness and consistency, in languages, there are a number of enhancements of words and sentence constructions. While in principle, languages can function without these enhancements, they help to reduce the necessary concentration effort on the part of the listener and immensely increase reading speed on the part of the reader. Here are some examples:

- **Writing Direction.** The writing convention of left-to-right direction (as in English) in comparison with right-to-left (as in Arabic) or top-to-bottom (as in Chinese) are not the only variations. In the earliest times, the Greeks even used to alternate the writing direction for successive lines (better readability), but later settled down to writing left to right (more standardized).

- **Omission.** Sentences can also be optimized, whether through more abstract expression, the omission of vowels (as with old Semitic languages) or the omission of blank spaces, periods, or commas.

- **Plural Form.** The plurals in Egyptian Arabic are formed by integrating the number and type of the thing being counted. The plural form specifies whether there are one, two, or many objects. There is also a distinction between masculine and feminine plurals, as well as separate constructions for genus collective nouns. The plural forms for "two apples" and "apples" (genus) are constructed differently.

- **Tenses.** Modifications of verbs which normally incorporate tense ("When does the change appear, or when did it appear?") and an indication of active or passive voice ("Is the subject the cause of the change?") represent only *optimizations* and are not an essential part of a complete language. In Chinese, for instance, this kind of verb modification (known as inflection) does not exist. Without tenses, we have to translate a statement such as "Yesterday I wanted to eat porridge, but there was no more milk" as "Yesterday I want eat porridge but yesterday I eat no porridge because yesterday there be no more milk."

- **Gender-specific pronouns.** With pronouns, we can refer to a subject or object mentioned earlier. In the sentence "Today, I have seen a dog; it had scraggly fur," the pronoun "it" replaces the word "dog." Of course, this optimization can lead to problems if we have to deal with multiple entities. In the sentence "The sun shines on the garden and it looks wonderful today," we do not know to what exactly the word "it" refers. Is it the garden or is it the sun that looks wonderful? We have to guess from the context. In the German language, this can sometimes be resolved because of gender-specific pronouns. In German, the sun is "female" ("*die* Sonne") but the garden is "male" ("*der* Garten"). So, we can refer to the garden as "he" and to the sun as "she," and either say "he looks wonderful," or "she looks wonderful," resolving the potential misunderstanding.

- **Gender-specific articles.** Interestingly, German articles carry a part of their culture in themselves. The propensity to personalize entities goes far back to ancient times where for example the Earth (female pronoun in German) was seen as the "mother" and the sky (male pronoun in German) was seen as having the role of the "father." People saw how the earth was "fertilized" by the sky—the rain—just as we were conceived ourselves. Thus, parts of our concept hierarchy find their way even into the *grammar* of our language. The influence of these seemingly small peculiarities of our language became apparent in a study. The participating German and Spanish native speakers (who were also fluent in English, a language with no grammatical gender system) were asked to describe different (English) words with a list of adjectives. "For example, the word 'key' is masculine in German and feminine in Spanish. German speakers described keys as *hard, heavy, jagged, metal, serrated,* and *useful,* while Spanish speakers said they were *golden, intricate, little, lovely, shiny,* and *tiny.* The word 'bridge,' on the other hand, is feminine in German and masculine in Spanish. German speakers described bridges as *beautiful, elegant, fragile, pretty, peaceful,* and *slender,* while Spanish speakers said they were *big, dangerous, long, strong, sturdy,* and *towering*."[10]

- **Adjectives and adverbs**: As for adjectives and adverbs, it should be noted that these likewise are used mostly in shortened form. Thus, by "a tall man" we actually mean "a taller-*than-average* man," i.e., we orient ourselves according to cultural norms, to the current average case, or to other entities in the current situation. Obviously, these forms of description are inexact since they depend on the context.

True complexity comes into play only when we place several entities in relation to one another in terms of their properties or, particularly, the time-related changes of individual properties. It is understandable that the ever-growing complexity of human civilization over time led to the development of linguistic optimizations. While at their foundation, even complex situations can be depicted without optimizations—because language, as its core, ultimately only depicts concepts, their properties, changes in these properties, and the relation between entities. But as a statement such as "Before I returned home from work yesterday, the burglar had already disappeared" demonstrates, with our modern language we can describe a situation which would be laborious to depict without optimization:

- The property "time" of the action "disappear" of the entity "burglar" was smaller than the property "time" of the action "return home from work" of the entity "I."

- The property "time" of the action "disappear" of the entity "burglar" and the property "time" of the action "return home from work" of the entity "I" correspond roughly to "yesterday."

---

[10]Boroditsky, Schmidt, and Phillips, *Sex, Syntax, and Semantics,* p. 70.

A last example can be found in our typeset itself. Our modern alphabet builds upon the Latin alphabet, which consists primarily of phonemes. In our language, however, the usefulness of special images was preserved for us in the form of ideograms such as numbers, the percent symbol (%), currency symbols, etc. In this respect, we have the best of both worlds: a universally intelligible alphabet on one hand, and as an optimization, ideograms standing for often-used concepts on the other.

> **Idea**
>
> Concept hierarchy aside, languages are basically trivial. Only including optimizations like time-related changes and pronouns makes them complex.

### 2.1.4 Learning of Languages

> **Question**
>
> How do children learn the concepts "past" and "future"?

The more frequently we experience a certain familiar situation, the more clearly we can identify the essential and inessential parts of the connection. If we want to teach a dog to sit on command, we must repeat the command until the dog sits on its own, after which we give it a reward. At that point, it does not yet understand the connection between the reward, the act of sitting, and the command. But through repetition in different situations and circumstances, after a few dozen times, it will have understood. It has then connected the reward, the act of sitting, and the command, and learned the concept "Sit!"

One important thing to note here, though, is that in order to use concepts, we actually need no language that is communicable to others. Simple relations can automatically (implicitly) be understood, e.g., one's orientation in space, how to peel a banana, how to swim in water, or how to satisfy our hunger. If we see a table, we need not think of the word "table" in order to recognize it. This has been tested by giving speech-impaired children the task of selecting three pictures out of seven that belong together. Obviously, this task can only be solved if you create underlying concepts and select the one that fits exactly to three of the pictures. For the pictures scale, pencil, stopwatch, refrigerator, wine glass, ruler, and skyscraper, you can find categories in which seven ("entity"), six ("appliances"), two ("office appliances"), or—the best answer—three ("measurement devices") pictures fit. A comparison with healthy children showed that while the speech-impaired were significantly weaker at age eight, they performed comparably by age 14. Thus, the lack of speech does not prevent the creation of concepts.[11] For our actions, for this reason, an implicit notion of underlying concepts will often suffice. We can understand (many) concepts without the ability to put them into spoken words. But actually, we *do* develop a kind of *internal* language that is difficult to communicate to others because it is very subjective: we achieve this with the very learning of a communicable language.

The understanding comes before the production of language. With understanding, we need only to *recognize* phonemes. It is at the beginning not yet important to have an exact definition. On the other hand, we have difficulties beginning with an exact thought and applying incompletely understood, ambiguous concepts. For instance, if a child uses words like car, ball, and house, it is by no means certain that she means the same thing as would an adult using these words. The child must first gradually learn where the boundaries of the meaning of a term lie. So, the onomatopoetic "doggy" could be "overstretched" and be used not only for dogs but also for all animals

---

[11]cf. Zimmer, *So kommt der Mensch zur Sprache*, p. 172.

with fur. Conversely, an "understretching" of the word would consist of its being used only for a certain dog or for dogs in a particular situation.

For children learning language, in order to understand the concepts "past," "present," and "future," two steps are necessary (see Figure 2.1). The concept "present" is relatively easy to understand—the referenced incident temporally correlates directly with the statement; all other time references will be interpreted as "not present." It only becomes clear in the second step that there is a deeper difference between "past" and "future."[12]

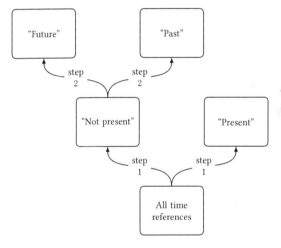

**Figure 2.1:** Two steps are required to understand the concepts "past" and "future."

Another point is that language (with the exception of accents) is not passed on through simple imitation; otherwise, we would hear children at least trying to speak in complex sentences. Rather, the speech of parents serves as a collection of aural "fingerprints" which the child learns and remembers. In addition, by taking note of the

---

[12]cf. Zimmer, *So kommt der Mensch zur Sprache*, pp. 49–51.

reactions to her use of the language, she learns to differentiate between right and wrong fingerprints. When she then formulates new sentences, the words are matched with and evaluated against these imprints in memory. Over time, the sentences that are formed by the child fit better and better with the memorized fingerprints: she learns the underlying grammar, i.e., that which connects all those fingerprints together. The significant difference between a child and an adult learning a language is that the children are usually missing the fear of making mistakes. This is the key to quickly learning a language. If you do not use it actively and instead strive for perfection from the beginning, then you are making it more difficult for yourself.[13]

---

**Did you know?**

In nature, different plant and animal species compete for the same living environment. Their success depends how well-adapted a species is to its surroundings. In the human brain, there are similar structures. There, different *thoughts* compete within an environment consisting of sense data and memories (like the aural "fingerprints" of language) to form a part of the consciousness.

$\longrightarrow$ Read more in *Philosophy for Heroes: Continuum*

---

Children who grow up in a multilingual environment are in a special position. They can acquire multiple languages as their mother tongue, although possibly with a limitation. If the languages are learned independent of the usual cultural environment, then this can lead to an erroneous use of the second language. For someone who has learned the language in its usual cultural context, these terms can mean something different and refer to different concepts. For example, just knowing that "democracy" literally translates into the German word "Demokratie" is only of little help because the un-

---

[13]cf. Zimmer, *So kommt der Mensch zur Sprache*, pp. 49–51.

derlying meaning of the word in Germany might be very different compared to the meaning in North America. That is why when we learn a second language, usually we not only learn new rules and new words, but we also learn new meanings in the context of a native speaker. The meaning of a word is related to the context in which it was learned. That is the reason someone who learns two languages in the same context does not acquire the finer differences in meaning. On the other hand, if both languages are learned in *different* environments, the chances to obtain a balanced form of bilingualism are the highest. From the usage of the language, it becomes apparent for the child to which context it refers.[14]

---

[14]cf. Zimmer, *So kommt der Mensch zur Sprache*, pp. 69–72.

## 2.2  Language and Mathematics

To those who do not know mathematics, it is difficult to get
across a real feeling as to the beauty, the deepest beauty, of
nature. [...] If you want to learn about nature, to appreciate
nature, it is necessary to understand the language that she
speaks in.

—Richard Feynman, *Character of Physical Law*

**Question**

Why did humankind develop a system of mathematics?

THE ORIGIN OF MATHEMATICS can be found most likely well before that of written language. With the centralization of communi-
ties (such as in the Sumerian kingdom, around 2300 BC), and with
job specialization, increasing population density, and stationary settlements, features of society such as calendar systems, astronomy,
trade, land surveying, work-sharing, storage of goods, and currency
gained importance. The more accurately a king knew the extent of
his land holdings, the more accurately he was able to tax them—just
as farmers could cultivate their fields more productively when they
knew exactly what calendar day it was, or as astronomers could better predict the movements of bodies in space when they learned concepts of geometry. These applications revolved particularly around
enumeration and measurements. Also, theories related to irrational
numbers already existed in Greek antiquity (ca. 500 BC), dealing explicitly with lengths of diagonals and implicitly with the application
of the "golden ratio" in the arts, but a scientifically sound definition
of irrational numbers, as well as the field of set theory, did not exist
until after the Renaissance, the heyday of mathematics.

> **Idea**
>
> Mathematics arose from the need to count quantities, to compare quantities, and to describe processes.

In the following, we will focus less on general mathematical history than on the coupling of language and the representation of entities. In particular focus, we will consider the question of what a "set" is, what a "number" is, and how and in what form we should use those concepts. The reason for this chapter is that in discussions, aspects of mathematics are often used wrongly as an ontological or epistemological argument. A clear understanding of what mathematics is, in relation to the philosophy that we have discussed so far, can help prevent or resolve misunderstandings.

### 2.2.1 Sets

> **Question**
>
> Sets are not, themselves, entities; what are they?

*Sets* are a central subject both in mathematics and in daily communication. The question is: What are sets? Do they exist? Do they have the properties of their elements? Is there an invisible tape that connects all elements? Let us first take a look at the different ways the term "set" is used:

- An enumeration of definite concepts, entities, or quantities of definite entities ("apples, pears, oranges," "these apples," "these three piles of apples")

- All entities belonging to a concept ("all apples")

- All entities defined by a recursion ("the natural numbers," "the rational numbers")

- All entities specifiable by an infinite generative process ("the irrational numbers")

- All self-referential sets ("the set of all sets")

According to our definitions of "entity" and "existence," sets are *not* entities since they do not have properties with which they could interact with entities. If you place five oranges together, you do not suddenly end up with more than five oranges.[15] An (unstructured) set never contains more members than those determined by the properties that define the set. The properties of a set are strictly mental constructs that describe its members.

Basically, sets correspond to concepts. The difference is that concepts are not defined as enumerations of entities, but rather as the enumeration of *properties* of entities. For example, the concept "chair" could be defined by the properties "chair legs," "seating," and "optionally a backrest," while we enumerate a set of three chairs for example by "this blue chair," "that green chair," and "that big chair over there." A given set could consist of only a portion of all existing entities of a concept (e.g., of *all existing* elements of a concept *except for one*), while concepts always refer to *all* existing associated entities (and entities that will be discovered in the future or that existed in the past).

For a better understanding, let us consider another set, namely "all people residing in New York." What exactly is this set? Would it be meaningfully defined or comprehensible if everyone were tied together with string? Or does this set correspond literally to the written sentence, the ink on the paper?

---

[15]Socks in washing machines are a famous exception: you might end up with less or more socks of the same or different colors and sizes.

It should be apparent that we need more in order to be able to intelligibly *grasp* and define this term. If we consider the set of New York residents, then we do not need to assemble millions of people in an office in order to deal with them. Rather, we deal with *pointers*, such as a list of telephone numbers or addresses.[16] Thus, we could *describe* the set of all New Yorkers for example in the form of a thick telephone book. As the sentence itself asserts, the telephone book itself is *not* the set—it simply *describes* the set; it tells you in an organized way who is part of the group "New York residents" and who is not.

> **SET** • A *set* is a pointer to a number of entities who share properties defined by the set (e.g., the set of the "Seven Seas" refer to the seven oceanic bodies of water of Earth, i.e., the four oceans and the three large Mediterranean seas). Put another way, sets are a way of organizing or grouping entities; they make life easier.

**Idea**

Sets are only *enumerations* of existing entities or other sets, not the entities themselves.

### 2.2.1.1 Set of all Sets

**Question**

Why can sets not contain themselves?

One counter-argument that is often brought up against rationality is the notion of the existence of the "set of all sets." Mathematics intro-

---

[16]Not everybody in New York has a telephone number or an address—if we really wanted to reach everyone, we would need to sound an alarm or drive around in a car with a loudspeaker. And then we would still need to send people into buildings to be really sure.

duces its own axiomatic system which (unlike Objectivism) places artificial "axioms" first, rather than reality or the individual. At this point, Gödel's theorem again becomes important: a system built upon axioms is necessarily either incomplete or inconsistent. Therefore, the fact that the construct "set of sets" can be defined, but due to its recursive definition (a recursive definition is a process, not an enumeration!) cannot exist, does not break with our considerations up to this point: mathematics can indeed (with recursion, if need be) describe any measurement ("complete"), but it is also possible to describe entities which cannot exist ("inconsistent").

---

*Example*

"Points" behave in a similar way in geometry (and the same holds for lines, cubes, etc.). Here again, we are dealing with representatives (pointers) because points do not exist; they are infinitely small, have no properties, and are representable in space only through imaginary relations and measurements.

---

**Idea**

Sets have to be countable and cannot contain themselves.

---

### 2.2.1.2 Countable Sets

> The simplest thought, like the concept of the number one, has an elaborate logical underpinning.

> —Carl Sagan, *Cosmos—The Lives of the Stars*

**Question**

Why is it that axiomatic systems in mathematics need not have a connection to reality?

In Chapter 1.5, "Ontology," we discussed basic truths of reality. The three axioms mentioned—of Existence, Identity, and Consciousness —constitute an *axiomatic system*:

> **AXIOMATIC SYSTEM** • An *axiomatic system* is the set of axioms that is the foundation of all knowledge within a field of study.

In mathematics, our discussion likewise deals with an axiomatic system. We now encounter the question of whether there could even be other axiomatic systems than that of Existence, Identity, and Consciousness. The axiomatic system of mathematics has arisen as a form of expression of measurements, which over time has become increasingly formalized. The more crucial *difference* between mathematical axioms and our axioms of philosophy is the fact that mathematics in most cases is practiced purely *rationalistically*. So the mathematical axioms used in it are *not* self-evident; they are only construed to facilitate particularly elegant depictions of numbers.

**Idea**

Axiomatic systems in mathematics need not have a connection to reality or be self-evident. They are purely rationalistic, self-contained systems.

The only limitation here is simply that the axioms of an axiomatic system cannot contradict one another (otherwise we could not create logical deductions of additional truths). There is an infinite number of such axiomatic systems. But as purely rationalistic constructs, they do not necessarily have to have a relation to reality (i.e., in a perception). A mathematical axiomatic system based on observations of reality would be a simple enumeration of situations and actions. For instance: "I have banana$_1$; I put banana$_2$ beside banana$_1$. Now I have banana$_1$ and banana$_2$." More complex statements or even general models of reality are not possible this way. Correspondingly, we have proceeded instead to attach mathematics to a system which is in itself free of contradictions.

**Question**

What are possible shortcomings of a recursive description of natural numbers?

A simple example of a system not based on empirical experience would be the abbreviated recursive definition of the natural numbers:

- 1 is a natural number;
- If $n$ is a natural number, then its successor is also; and
- 1 is never a successor.

By this definition, the statement "3 is a natural number" is true: 3 is the successor of 2, 2 is the successor of 1, and 1 is a natural number. These "axioms" thus do not contradict one another, but they are also simply plucked out of the air since they can be set up without any connection to reality. Here, the number 1 does not stand for an entity, but rather represents a *measurement* of the number of entities. On its own, a number is not an illustration of an entity or a set of entities. If we want to apply mathematical results in reverse, we must again allocate real entities to this abstraction. Consider the following example:

> **Example**
>
> You would like to buy three bananas for your children. It
> makes no difference to them which bananas they are, as long
> as they have certain properties, that is, they can be allocated
> to the concept "banana." Hence, the children would not ac-
> cept an apple. It also makes no difference to them which child
> receives which particular banana.

Correspondingly, you would not say to the fruit merchant, "I want
this banana for Tom, this one for Amelia, and this one for Peter"—
you would simply say that you want to buy three bananas. From
this statement, the fruit merchant does not know which banana is
for which child, but he does not need to know—this shows the great
power of abstract thinking: we save a lot of time by avoiding or
disregarding specific cases. Conversely, the fruit merchant makes
a measurement instead of asking you which banana you want. For
this, he places the three bananas one after the other in a basket.
Thus, he has concretized the mathematical result of the calculation
and allocated three real entities.

Also, if we follow a number with successor after successor, we can
arrive at arbitrarily large numbers. But this does not mean that
something like "infinity" would have suddenly gained a foothold in
reality as an entity. The axioms of the natural numbers describe a
*process* whereby we can count any quantity of entities. But the fact
that we *can* count up to a certain number does not mean that a corresponding quantity of entities actually exists in reality. Returning
to our previous example, if you had asked for ten thousand bananas,
the fruit merchant probably would not have been able to fulfill this
request—such a number would not be available, even though the
mathematics we defined allows us to ask for it. Thus, a systematic,
logical mathematician (a rationalist) would get into conflict with reality time after time if he did not use sound common sense, i.e., if

he did not translate the complete language of mathematics into a consistent one.

To illustrate, we cannot infer that if there are 10 oranges, there must also be an 11th or if it even makes sense to speak of 11 oranges. Think about other concepts such as days, spaces on a chess board, or truth values, whose quantities are all countable, while the natural numbers are countable but potentially *infinitely* so. A mixture of both forms of numbers can lead to errors if, for example, invalid values are entered in a form (e.g., the date "February 30," or in chess, "move pawn to position space $s_{11}$"—there is neither such a date on the calendar, nor such a position on the board). These errors indeed intuitively appear obvious to us, but in complex statements or philosophical systems this oversight can quickly escape us, which is why we have to be very precise in the wording of our definitions.

An erroneous mixture of complete and consistent systems also impedes us in our thinking. For example, if we regard the truth values *True* and *False* erroneously as a quantity (and assign the number 1 to True and 0 to False) instead of a set, we could ask ourselves whether there could also be a third or fourth truth value (like half-truth, quarter-truth, etc.) between or beyond 0 and 1. This question does not result from an observation of reality, but from a gap which is open because of our complete but inconsistent language. Just because we can enumerate entities of a set does not mean that it makes sense to ask what happens with larger quantities. Just because we have "1" life and just because we can count to 9, does not mean that it makes sense to ask about our lives "2" to "9."[17] Thus, such "mathematical" questions need to be checked first to ensure they make sense before investing any time solving them.

---

[17] It comes to no surprise that this representation of reality can be found in computer games anyways. The underlying mathematical description of the computer simulation basically seduces the game designer to do it this way.

> **Idea**
>
> The recursive description of natural numbers indeed supplies a complete picture of reality, but, unfortunately, it is a potentially erroneous picture.

> **Question**
>
> Why is mathematics not simply a science of entities?

As we established in Chapter 2.1.2, "Completeness and Consistency," according to Gödel's Incompleteness Theorem, axiomatic systems are necessarily either incomplete or inconsistent. As shown above, the recursive definition of the natural numbers indeed supplies a complete picture of reality ("complete"), but, unfortunately, a potentially erroneous picture, as there are (theoretical) representations of numbers which have no counterparts in reality ("inconsistent"). So, we have our philosophical axiomatic system (that is based on self-evident truths, i.e., it is *consistent*) on the one side, and the mathematical axiomatic system (that is constructed in a way as to be *complete*) on the other side. For this reason, mathematics ultimately is *not* the science of entities (like our consistent philosophical axiomatic system is), but rather principally the science of *relations* of entities, that is to say, *measurements* of their properties.

> **Idea**
>
> Mathematics is *not* the science of entities, but rather principally the science of *relations* of entities, that is to say, *measurements* of their properties.

## 2.2.2 Ratios

An extension of the natural numbers are the so-called *rational numbers*, which we can generate recursively using the "Diagonal Argument" using the natural numbers, i.e. they are infinite but countable, exactly like the natural numbers. A rational number is thereby the ratio of two natural numbers, so from the outset it has nothing directly to do with a real, existing entity; rather, it is purely a mental concept which refers to a *relation* between entities.

The term "half of an apple" does not indicate an apple with a property of "half-ness" (as in the case of half of an apple hanging on a tree), but rather it should emphasize the temporal relation—the life history—of the apple: it was once whole and now has been halved. Alternatively, we can see this term as an instruction for the creation of the entity, the "recipe" for a half of an apple: "Take an apple and divide it." Hence, if we use numbers and general mathematics, and we wish to forge a connection to reality, we should keep the idea of constructibility in mind.

---

*Example*

We could rack our brain for a long time trying to figure out why a division by zero makes no sense. In light of our previous explanation, the cause becomes apparent: rational numbers do not always correctly depict reality, since their definition only refers to a relation *between* entities and not entities themselves. And since "nothing" is not an entity, division by zero is not constructible.

> **Did you know?**
>
> Mathematicians are divided on the issue whether con-
> structibility—the so-called mathematical constructivism—is
> relevant for mathematical objects. This becomes important
> when discussing physics. Is it possible to follow insights
> about reality from mathematical relationships?
>
> $\longrightarrow$ Read more in *Philosophy for Heroes: Continuum*

### 2.2.3 Irrational Numbers

Just as the introduction of the irrational numbers [...] is a convenient myth [which] simplifies the laws of arithmetic [...] so
physical objects are postulated entities which round out and
simplify our account of the flux of existence [...] The concep-
tional scheme of physical objects is [likewise] a convenient
myth, simpler than the literal truth and yet containing that
literal truth as a scattered part.

—Willard Van Orman Quine, *On What There Is*

> **Question**
>
> If the circle circumference is "irrational," does this mean that
> there are no circles in reality? How do irrational numbers
> appear in nature?

The term "irrational" suggests that there is something in the universe located outside of our perception and our mind. It is true that we cannot represent the circumference of a circle using a natural number or a ratio of two natural numbers. Irrational numbers are infinite and uncountable since they, unlike the rational numbers, cannot be constructed from the natural numbers in a finite number of steps.

---

### Idea

Irrational numbers do not refer to quantities or ratios and do not appear in nature as such. Instead, they refer to processes, or methods of generation (circles, golden ratio, leaf arrangements, proportions, etc.).

---

### Question

What aspect of nature is the source of its complexity?

---

We have already seen that rational numbers deal with an abstraction, namely relations between entities and their properties. With irrational numbers, the method of generation is simply one or more steps of abstraction deeper; so we are no longer dealing with abstractions, but rather with the results of measurements of properties of entities.

For the calculation of the circumference of a circle, we select a point with the distance of the circle radius from the center of the circle and then make infinitely many, infinitely small steps, changing our angle with each step by a correspondingly infinitely small value, so that we always travel around the center point at a distance equal to the radius. When we add the distances together, we obtain the value of the circumference.

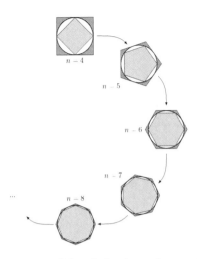

**Figure 2.2:** Approximation of the circle circumference through polygons from the inside and outside

But in practice, this method is not useful. While we would get an exact result, an infinite amount of time would be required to reach it. If we walk instead a *finite* amount of steps around the center of the circle, we get an *approximation* of the circumference. Figure 2.2 shows such an approximation with different polygons with an increasing number of corners within and outside the circle. A circle itself would constitute a polygon with "infinite corners." This construction was first calculated and proven in the third century BC by Archimedes.

As this method of construction suggests, there can be, for example, no "circumference of a circle" amount of apples. A number can be constructed in completely different ways: just because something looks like a number does not mean that you can use it like an *amount* of entities. A number which represents a ratio is something completely different than a number which represents an amount. This is the reason it is important to use numbers in the right context and to know how they were constructed in the first place.

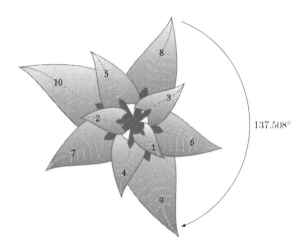

**Figure 2.3:** Optimal leaf arrangement

One conclusion from the fact that irrational numbers cannot be expressed as a relation (i.e., ratio) between natural numbers is that a multiplication of an irrational number by a chosen natural number always results in another irrational number. At first, this sounds like mathematical thought gimmickry, but upon closer inspection, we discover that *nature* makes extensive use of this quite abstract property.

The fundamental problem that a plant must overcome during its growth process is to get as much sunlight as possible on its leaves. If the leaves are arranged according to a regular (i.e., rational) pattern, such as "Leaf / quarter-turn / leaf / quarter-turn, ..." the leaves will overshadow one another. The solution is to find an angle of rotation which can be continuously repeated so that no two leaves grow directly above one another (see Figure 2.3).

Nature's solution is the so-called "golden ratio," which can be calculated to arbitrarily high accuracy by the Fibonacci number sequence by the simplest means. In the case of plants, this number sequence is generated through cell division with a simple rule: "Each mature cell divides and new cells require a certain length of time to mature." The process would occur as follows:

- From the new cell develops a mature cell. [1]

- From the mature cell develops a mature cell and a new cell. [2]

- From the mature cell develops a mature cell and a new cell, and from the new cell develops a mature cell. [3]

- From the two mature cells develops two mature cells and two new cells, and from the new cell develops a mature cell. [5]

- From the three mature cells develops three mature cells and three new cells, and from the two new cells develop two mature cells. [8]

- Etc.

As this sequence propagates, the Fibonacci sequence is generated: "1, 1, 2, 3, 5, 8, 13, 21, 34," etc., whereby the ratio of two successive numbers gives an increasingly accurate value of the golden ratio (1.618033...):

$$\frac{3}{2} = 1.5; \frac{5}{3} = 1.\overline{6}; \frac{8}{5} = 1.6; \frac{13}{8} = 1.625; \frac{21}{13} = 1.6153\ldots$$

If we divide a complete rotation by this golden ratio, we obtain a series of angle values that minimize overlaps between leaves and thus maximize the amount of sunlight the plant can absorb.

If we draw squares using the Fibonacci numbers as the lengths of sides, we obtain the "golden spiral" (see Figure 2.4), which can be found in snails and flowers (see Figure 2.5).

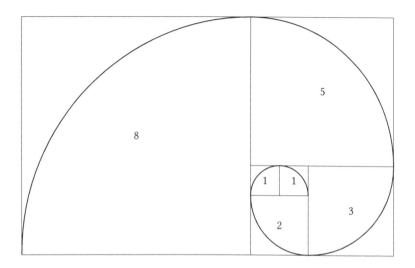

**Figure 2.4:** Fibonacci spiral with Fibonacci numbers

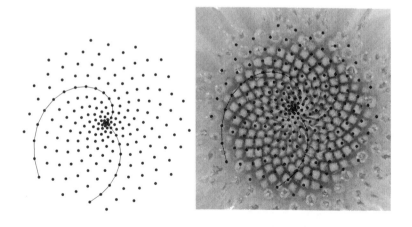

**Figure 2.5:** Fibonacci spirals in a chamomile flower

We conclude that irrational numbers do not represent quantities of elements but instead are indicative of a very specific infinite *process*. The infinite process of describing a circle in terms of an $n$-sided polygon enables us to express the irrational number $\pi$; the infinite process of generating the Fibonacci number sequence is reflected in the golden ratio, and so on. The fact that we can speak about irrational numbers does not mean that reality is irrational—those are two completely different matters.

> **Idea**
>
> The complexity of reality stems from the fact that it is a *product* of infinitely repeating processes.

> **Did you know?**
>
> This golden ratio can be commonly found throughout nature (including human bodies). Likewise, our own perception is "calibrated" to find objects displaying this ratio to be particularly appealing.
>
> $\longrightarrow$ Read more in *Philosophy for Heroes: Act*

## 2.2.4 Mathematics and Empiricism

> The real problem in speech is not *precise* language. The problem is *clear* language. The desire is to have the idea clearly communicated to the other person. It is only necessary to be precise when there is some doubt as to the meaning of a phrase, and then the precision should be put in the place where the doubt exists. It is really quite impossible to say anything with absolute precision, unless that thing is so abstracted from the real world as to not represent any real thing.

—Richard Feynman, *New Textbooks for the New Mathematics*

**Question**

What is the relationship between counting and philosophy?

If we gave an empiricist the (apparently simple) task of copying several lines from one sheet of paper to another by hand, he would be faced with a formidable problem: without the capability of counting, he has problems similar to those we would face if we had to draw a lawn. Would you start counting each blade of grass and then count again up to that number when making your own brush strokes? No, you would simply paint an area that just *looks like* a lawn—regardless of how the individual blades of grass actually are standing. And likewise, for an empiricist, a number of lines is but an image. He would not copy the lines from one paper to the other but draw a *representation* of "a number of lines."[18,19]

---

[18]cf. Holden, *How Language Shapes Math.*
[19]cf. Everett, *Recursion and Human Thought: Why the Piraha Don't Have Numbers.*

> **Idea**
>
> Counting is not a trivial capability or an innate one, but rather a deeply internalized expression of a system of philosophy learned early in life and embodied in language and culture.

Therefore, for the reasons discussed, there can be no mathematics in a purely empirically (i.e., in terms of empiricism) interpreted language, as quantities refer to recurrent concepts.[20] What we can learn from empiricists, though, is that we should not confuse numbers with entities. "One orange" is something principally different than "this orange here." It is easy to mistake a *measurement* ("one") of the number of entities of a concept ("orange") with the actual entities ("this orange"). When an empiricist looks at a basket with six bananas, he cannot see 6 bananas. What he sees is the whole picture, this banana, that banana, that banana over there, etc. There is no plural for an empiricist. All he could do about the bananas is compare them to another experience he had, e.g., there are "'more / less than usual' banana" or "'about as much as yesterday' banana." For him, each entity stands on its own and cannot be subsumed under a concept. Accordingly, for him there can be no word for "all;" that would certainly refer to concepts—all entities of this concept that exist somewhere. The difference between enumerations and measurements becomes important in the following section when we take a look at the number *zero*.

---

[20]cf. Everett, *Das glücklichste Volk—Sieben Jahre bei den Pirahã-Indianern am Amazonas*, p. 199.

## 2.2.5 The Zero

While there already was a depiction of zero in ancient Babylon about 4,000 years ago, they simply used it as a delimiter between individual numerals, like in our system the zero in, e.g., the number 101. At the end of the number, though, no zeros were added. If we applied this to our number system, it would be unclear whether the number 1 meant 1, 10, 100, or 1000. Here, you had to guess the scale from the context.

In the Roman numeral system, all numerals had to be added together, a system well suited for smaller numbers. With the calculation of distances in space by Indian astronomers in the 9th century, introducing the numeral 0 as well as the positional notation (e.g., 123 was no longer $1 + 2 + 3 = 6$ but instead $1 * 100 + 2 * 10 + 3 * 1 = 123$) was required. This idea found its way from India to Europe by way of Arabic scholars and traders which is the reason why we, when speaking of our numerals, (erroneously) speak of "Arabic numerals" today (see Figure 2.6). Zero as its own *digit* was introduced in Europe only in the 12th century by Leonardo Bonacci (also known as *Fibonacci*).

| European | 0 | 1 | 2 | 3 | 4 | 5 | 6 | 7 | 8 | 9 |
|---|---|---|---|---|---|---|---|---|---|---|
| Arabic-Indian | ٠ | ١ | ٢ | ٣ | ٤ | ٥ | ٦ | ٧ | ٨ | ٩ |
| Eastern Arabic-Indiah (Persian and Urdu) | ٠ | ١ | ٢ | ٣ | ۴ | ۵ | ۶ | ۷ | ۸ | ۹ |
| Devanagari (Hindi) | ० | १ | २ | ३ | ४ | ५ | ६ | ७ | ८ | ९ |
| Tamil | | ௧ | ௨ | ௩ | ௪ | ௫ | ௬ | ௭ | ௮ | ௯ |

**Figure 2.6:** Indian origin of our numbers

**Question**

Does "zero" have an equivalent in reality? If you have "zero" apples and "zero" lemons, is what you have (in terms of apples and lemons) the same?

Zero as an independent *number* was first actively used in Europe after the 17th century to apply to measurements of scales (temperature, sea level, etc.). With the emergence of rationalism and the desire to make a complete language out of mathematics, people integrated the number zero into existing number systems. From this, besides the problem of division by zero, there arose the question of what, e.g., "0 apples" means. What is the difference between "0 apples" and "0 pears"? What exactly happens if I buy "0 cows for 0 coins"?

When we consider the *number* zero today, we must keep this narrative in the back of our minds. Zero as a *numeral* is a blank space, and zero as a *number* is a measurement. To understand the concept of zero, you have to understand the difference between enumerations and measurements. If you point at a group of cows ("these five cows"), it is called an enumeration. If we notice that three cows are missing, it is a measurement ("minus 3 cows"). If we know that the cows named Berta, Elfriede, and Anja are missing, it is again an enumeration. Thus, the zero can never be an *enumeration* because we can neither point at it nor name it. That is the reason dividing the cake by zero guests does not work; a division by zero is forbidden in mathematics. The occurrence of a division by zero points to a deeper flaw in our understanding of the task in question: a confusion between an enumeration and a measurement. Thus, arguments that are substantiated by the *number* zero (or the "nothingness") have to be examined extra carefully.

**Idea**

The *digit* "0" originally served merely as a blank space, while the *number* "0" has no identity and thus no equivalent in reality but can only represent the result of a measurement and is mostly used as a form of negation. You could count an infinite list of things that you own 0 items of, without ever making progress to describe *what* you own.

## 2.2.6 Mathematics and Reality

**Question**

What are some of the limits of mathematics in terms of describing reality?

| Philosophy | Mathematics |
|---|---|
| entities | sets |
| potential entities | natural numbers |
| relations of entities | rational numbers |
| infinite processes | irrational numbers |

**Figure 2.7:** Comparison of philosophical and mathematical terms

We can compare mathematics with the philosophy of entities (see Figure 2.7). Thus, mathematics can only be used as a language to communicate mathematical results. Mathematics itself has no direct relation to entities, mathematics only describes the *relations and proportions of entities to each other*, i.e., *measurements* of properties and enumerations. This missing connection to reality means that mathematics on its own cannot be used for philosophical statements. Also, even though mathematics can lead to new results in physics, this does *not* mean that reality is *built upon* mathematics. We cannot use a mathematical finding (e.g., the "existence" of irrational numbers) to then conclude something about reality. The fact that we can construct a perfect circle in an infinite number of steps and describe this *process* with an irrational number $\pi$ does not mean that we live in an incomprehensible, "irrational" world.

**Did you know?**

To understand nature, it is not enough to perceive entities. The understanding of *processes* is a prerequisite to grasp concepts like science, consciousness, evolution, and quantum mechanics.

$\longrightarrow$ Read more in *Philosophy for Heroes: Continuum*

**Idea**

Reality is without contradiction. Mathematics is a good *tool* to describe measurements of reality. But a "nice" mathematical model that reflects the results of measurements exactly still remains a *model* and is not necessarily a description of reality.

## 2.3  The Value of Language

 Concepts and, therefore, language are primarily a tool of cognition—not of communication, as is usually assumed. Communication is merely the consequence, not the cause nor the primary purpose of concept-formation—a crucial consequence, of invaluable importance to men, but still only a consequence. Cognition precedes communication; the necessary precondition of communication is that one have something to communicate.

—Ayn Rand, *Introduction to Objectivist Epistemology*

THE BASIC PROPERTIES of language are now known to us. We also have examined the different categories of languages. We know what we have to look for and can begin to actually use language. But what is the value of language? Why is it so important?

### 2.3.1  The Foundation of Knowledge

As we have already established, learning an audible (or generally, communicable) language is *not* required for the origination and use of (simple) concepts. We can implicitly *grasp* what material objects are (there is a reason that babies learn through "grasping," i.e., "touching" objects—and chewing) and create concepts within our inner language. But whenever we must consciously realize a logical step (in thought or on paper) in order to draw further conclusions from it, a form of communicable language is indispensable. The simplest example would be the system of numbers. While we can intuitively grasp perhaps five, six, or seven elements without counting them, with the language of mathematics we have a tool and its hierarchical structure and recursive processes equip us to examine extremely large and complex problems.

> ### Example
>
> Think about your favorite piece of music, hum it, note by note, verse by verse. *Simple, isn't it?* Now imagine the whole piece of music *completely* in your mind, *not* just note by note or verse by verse. Try to remember a book that you have read. *Simple, isn't it?* Now try to imagine the book in its *totality* in your mind.

The average person can be conscious of a handful of elements at the same time. Without the use of images and concept hierarchies, which tie together a complex situation—which ultimately constitutes the essence of language—we quickly reach the limits of our own powers of concentration. The concretization and organization of our thoughts permits us to think about these concepts explicitly and consciously, and to delimit them grammatically using definitions. It also allows us to use them in connection with other concepts in combinations of potential unlimited complexity—in other words, to construct a hierarchy of knowledge. We walk from one concept to the next connected one without having to worry about keeping both in our mind.

Without language, thoughts and reflections of higher complexity are impossible. If we did not have language to begin with, effectively, we would first have to invent it since language is really the organization of knowledge into categories using entities and their relationships.

**Did you know?**

There are a few extraordinary individuals in any number of fields who can memorize long series of numbers, notes, and facts. Some make use of mnemonics, in the form of hierarchies, concepts, images, and optimizations (in other words, language!); others are often referred to as *savants*. For some, the brain area that deals with math is more strongly connected than usual to the brain area that handles visual information. They can see numbers as geometrical shapes or as colors, making calculations or memory exercises easier.

$\longrightarrow$ Read more in *Philosophy for Heroes: Continuum*

## 2.3.2 The Theory of Mind

**Question**

What is an example of a fourth order of intentionality?

**THEORY OF MIND** • The *theory of mind* refers to the cognitive skill that makes it possible to understand that another individual may have beliefs and desires that are different from one's own.

The difference between thinking and speaking also becomes clear when being asked to repeat what someone has said; a listener will rarely do this verbatim, but will instead express what he or she understood to be the thought behind the utterance. Simply said, if thinking and speaking were identical, neither effort nor any special ability would be needed to bring the two into agreement.[21] This is the ability to understand that another individual may have beliefs and desires that are different from one's own, i.e., to see the need to share something you already know in order for others to know

---

[21] cf. Zimmer, *So kommt der Mensch zur Sprache*, p. 167.

it, too. Apes may lack this ability, which may constrain their ability to acquire language—as is the case with very young children before their *theory of mind* abilities have developed.[22]

**Did you know?**

What about the case where a person simply wants to share something by speaking? An example is the bonding of parent and child. Without a theory of mind, the parent would have no model of what the child knows or does not know, and would tragically assume that the child already shared the parent's knowledge. While the parent could still display an emotional reaction, it might not be expressed with the conscious idea of letting the child know that he is loved. We, having this ability, take it for granted, but it is no trivial matter at all. That being said, people have different preferences. Some might prefer words, others might prefer actions as a sign of friendship or love. In that regard, there could be a theory of emotion, too. Without it, we might not be aware that the other person does not necessarily feel the way we do (or even knows how we feel).

⟶ Read more in *Philosophy for Heroes: Act*

"While a mother ape 'knows' how to crack nuts open with hammerstones, she cannot appreciate that her infant lacks that knowledge. So she has no incentive either to 'explain,' by gestures or calls, how it is done or to manipulate her infant to do it. If one assumes that another individual has the same knowledge and intentions as one's own, there is no need to communicate that knowledge or to manipulate their behavior. [...] If I know what I think, then I am termed as having a single order of intentionality; if I know what someone else thinks, then I have two orders of intentionality; if I know what someone else thinks what I am thinking, then I have three orders of

---

[22] cf Mithen, *The Singing Neanderthals—the Origins of Music, Language, Mind, and Body*, p. 23.

intentionality—and so forth. Whereas humans routinely use three or four orders of intentionality in their social lives, apes might be limited to two orders at the most."[23] This is the reason that language plays such a big role in our lives but not in the lives of apes.

> *Example*
>
> Female cats show a behavior that very much reminds us about the "theory of mind": they bring living prey to their kittens so that they can practice the hunting and killing of animals. While the mother does adapt to the abilities of her kittens, no deliberate teaching can be observed. She does not seem to try to understand her kittens in other situations than the hunt. Thus, the behavior has to be explained in a different way than with humans (cf. Cheney and Seyfarth, *How Monkeys See the World: Inside the Mind of Another Species*, pp. 223–24).

---

[23] Mithen, *The Singing Neanderthals—the Origins of Music, Language, Mind, and Body*, p. 117.

### 2.3.3 Language as Communication

**Question**

What are the three most significant obstacles in our communication with others?

An exchange of knowledge between two minds can occur directly through demonstration, as with apes learning the use of tools from one another through observation. The limit of this approach, of course, is that the teacher must always be present. If we want to point out to someone a food source located elsewhere, without language, there remains no other choice than to lead him to it ourselves.

The solution to the problem of needing an ever-present teacher is to create an abstraction, replacing the sensory perception (e.g., leading the person to the place) with an image. Besides describing it with spoken language, we could, instead of leading someone to an apple tree, *point* in the direction of the tree and give our counterpart an apple that we picked there. We could even dance like honey bees to tell which way to go. They communicate information to other bees in the hive, such as the distance to a nearby meadow, in which direction they must fly, and how much nectar can be found there. Another example can be seen with ants that mark the way to food sources with chemical scents—likewise a valid language, as the scent and its dispersion are a type of image representing the food source and the path to get there.

Thus, the first step in *communication* is that the participants find common ground. It needs to be clear which *image* represents which concept. In doing so, the foundation is laid by means of common experiences. The aforementioned "pointing" places an object and the person in relation and conveys this information to our counterpart in a clear, comprehensible form. Figure 2.8 shows the process of a conversation. Lisa has seen Peter in a crowd (sense data, sense perception, integration) and now illustrates this information in the form of text in a letter to Klaus. Klaus reads the letter (sense data, sense perception) and infers from the image (the text, i.e., the integration) that Lisa has seen Peter. Formally, communication can be defined as follows:

> **COMMUNICATION** • *Communication* is the attempt of an entity $A$ to translate knowledge (whether real or invented) of a situation through language into images and linguistic auxiliary structures, so that another entity $B$ can translate the series of images and linguistic auxiliary structures into knowledge of a situation perceived by $A$, without itself having obtained immediate sense data from the entities participating in the situation.

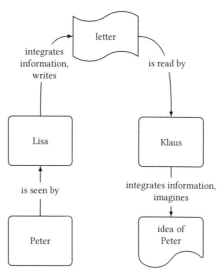

**Figure 2.8:** Example of the process of communication when using images (written text)

Unfortunately, there will be obstacles to our communication. The argument often arises in discussions, that everyone lives in his or her own world of experiences, and so we could not *objectively* communicate any concepts with our language. Is it possible that our sense data depends on our own personality or physical makeup and that every person can see the world only subjectively? Also, language has undergone changes over time and will continue to do so in the future. Thus, are we really allowed to say that we can communicate *objectively*?

Let us take a step back and concentrate on the core issue: Communication by means of language is ultimately the attempt of two conscious beings to become aware of the same entity and its condition (or, a situation comprising many entities and their conditions and relationships). To accomplish this, the following prerequisites have to be met:

- We have to share the same concept hierarchy and definitions.
- We need to be aware of cultural differences.
- We need to be aware of physiological differences (sense organs, brain, etc.); and
- We need to be able to trust our conversation partner to be willing to understand and tell the truth.

But finally, we need to have different perceptions of reality. While we could still exchange words with each other and look like we were communicating, we would not communicate anything (new). A society where differences are not appreciated does not communicate despite everyone talking.

## 2.3.3.1 Differences in Concepts

> **Question**
>
> What is the importance of corresponding definitions in a discussion?

A popular assumption is that the same words convey the same meanings. This is generally only correct if both conversation partners belong to a common *language network*, i.e., that they define their terms either among themselves or through close acquaintances.[24] The most obvious evidence for this is the fact that different languages predominate in different regions of the world. The greatest influences on our language are thus our direct communication partners, with whom we share common experiences. The less directly communication occurs, the fewer commonalities we have experienced through our cultures, the more difficult communication becomes—even if we speak the same language.

Without shared terms, problems occur especially in those subjects where we also do not have a direct, shared relation to reality. For example, a concept like "mind" has a culturally influenced history with a very specific meaning and interpretation, unlike the concept of "hand," which has changed little over time.[25]

If we cannot rely on a common language network, we need to create such a common basis. Particularly when communicating with unfamiliar people, be it in open discussions of any kind, through writing, in a conference, or on the Internet, it is, therefore, important to relate our own, learned definitions to our counterpart at the outset

---

[24] Interesting to note here is the theory that every person in the world is connected to every other person by approximately seven intermediate connections (cf. Travers et al., *An Experimental Study of the Small World Problem*).

[25] cf. Zimmer, *So kommt der Mensch zur Sprache*, p. 232.

and to ask for and agree on common definitions. There are of course dictionaries and legal texts which attempt to create a common standard for all people living in the domain of a particular language, but these also contain inexact or even conflicting definitions which can quickly lead to misunderstandings, especially in philosophical and political discussions.

**Idea**

Before we run hot-headed into a discussion about, e.g., God, democracy, equality, or freedom, we must ask our discussion partner for the corresponding definitions.

*Example*

There are also strictly hierarchical language networks, which are established and maintained through marketing by large companies and which often take a somewhat different form, since they are oriented toward economic power rather than communication between individuals. But, in this case, for the most part, only single terms (mainly trade names) are introduced into our language. Apple's "iPhone" has the same name everywhere; this label was assigned from the top down while there are many different designations for "smartphones" in general.

## 2.3.3.2  Cultural Differences

Even if we have learned all the definitions and the whole concept hierarchy of another person, our culture could still influence our thought and make mutual understanding difficult. Can we translate one concept from one language into another if we have significantly different cultural values?

When comparing our culture with others, we see what significant influence it can have on our thinking. In cultures where you cannot rely on structures of mutual trust that have been growing over centuries, abstract logic is valued differently. For example, illiterate rice farmers in West Africa were posed the following problem: "All men of your tribe are rice farmers. Mr. Smith is not a rice farmer. Is Mr. Smith a member of your tribe?"

Their answer was: "I don't know the man in person. I have not laid eyes on the man himself. [...] If I know him in person, I can answer that question, but since I do not know him in person, I cannot answer that question."[26] After the simplest kind of education, essentially consisting of memorization, there will be no more responses like that. At that point, people can interpret it as an abstract problem and solve it deductively without involving their own experience. But with unschooled, indigenous peoples, language merely serves as a communicative tool about the concrete, the obvious, and only that which is immediately accessible to personal experience.[27]

We have to note here, though, that the farmers do not necessarily think *illogically*. They might have simply a more comprehensive view on the subject, and their terms are less sharply defined because of their way of life. Also, we can assume that it is of great significance to the farmers who belongs to the tribe and who does not, so

---

[26] cf. Scribner, *Modes of thinking and ways of speaking.*
[27] cf. Zimmer, *So kommt der Mensch zur Sprache*, p. 265.

they do not want to rely on hearsay and instead choose to evaluate it personally. In addition, the first sentence—"All men of your tribe are rice farmers"—is probably not taken as an absolute by the farmers—as opposed to scientists in the realm of mathematics. What exactly one understands with the word "all" can be very different. "All"—in the sense of the person who poses the question—means "all all," i.e., everyone without exception. For the rice farmers, "all" might simply mean "all who I know" or "all who I see." Maybe you can become a member of the tribe by marriage. Maybe there are relatives outside of the village. Or maybe there are tribe rituals only through which you can become an official member of the tribe.

To conclude, before we judge another person's cognitive or linguistic abilities, we also need to be conscious of differences in culture. In most of the cases, we have to assume that—even in the case of very illogical looking answers—the other person, based on his available information, culture, and values, thinks logically. To actually translate a language, we not only have to try to match others' words and definitions to our own, but also we have to understand the world view of our conversation partner. If we judge another person based on his statements without regard to his culture, we might lose the best ally we have in our conversation partner: if we attack another's very cognitive faculty of logic, what other means are left for us to explain our point of view in a way the other person can comprehend?

## 2.3.3.3 Translatability

> **Question**
>
> How do languages differ in terms of expressiveness?

As we clarified in the introduction, the foundation of language is relatively simple, and its complexity stems mostly from the use of optimizations. Thus, we can assume that there has been an evolution of language, so (modern) language itself represents a (highly developed) cultural artifact. We can conclude that we also *think* with a different level of effectiveness depending on our language and the environment we use it in. If we can condense complex statements about relations into a short, pithy sentence, then the information can be memorized and mentally worked with more easily. Correspondingly, it could be difficult to translate the optimizations of one language into the other.

> **Idea**
>
> Differences between languages regarding their expressiveness concern only the length, accuracy, and clarity of their sentences.

> **Question**
>
> Why can no (complete) language prevent you from expressing a certain idea?

We are free to think about the limits of our language. But as soon as we try to take hold of our swirling thoughts and shape them into a communicable form, we necessarily fall back on our repertoire of terms and the grammar of our language. And conversely, in fields where our language already provides us with complete expressions, it is easier to think and express our thoughts. Thus, our language influences our thinking insofar as it takes more time and energy to think about things our language was not designed for.

This leads us to the *Sapir-Whorf hypothesis*, which states that our thought process and therefore our world view are (strongly) influenced by the grammar and vocabulary of the language we use.[28] As a consequence it is claimed that a language cannot be translated directly into another without error. As we have seen, however, more complex contexts are universally expressible in any language, provided that the language is entity-based. In addition, in case of doubt, we can always redefine a missing or differently defined concept in the translation or explain the differences.

> **SAPIR-WHORF HYPOTHESIS (WEAK VERSION)** • The *weak version* of the *Sapir-Whorf hypothesis* states that our language influences our thoughts, making it easier or harder to think or express certain ideas; different languages influence thoughts in different ways, so different languages contribute to different styles of thinking.

> **SAPIR-WHORF HYPOTHESIS (STRONG VERSION)** • The *strong version* of the *Sapir-Whorf hypothesis* states that our language determines our thinking; different languages make certain trains of thought possible or impossible in the first place. There is no general translatability of languages.

What the hypothesis ultimately deals with is the question of the relationship between concept and definition. A text *obviously* loses information in translation if it deals with *measurements*; for example, colors naturally depend on cultural perception, the allocation of color names to *measurement* values. With certain colors there are ways to calibrate these terms, as with the "color of blood." But

---

[28]cf. Zimmer, *So kommt der Mensch zur Sprache*, pp. 188–189.

other colors in the spectrum may not be available in the respective language culture, such as the rare and expensive purple during antiquity (which is why it is connected with nobility). We still find this very characteristic of the languages of primitive cultures; in the case of the Pirahã, there are no words for specific colors, but instead comparisons like "it has a color like blood," or wood, grass, etc.

Terms for concepts, on the other hand, can always be translated. The requirement is simply that the culture, in its use of language, acts realistically and does not see, for example, dogs and cars as being the same concept. If the concept in question is not yet understood in the other language, or if special cases are disregarded, then we can rewrite this concept on the basis of the existing definitions of more general concepts and so effectively define the missing term for the first time. There will not be a term for ultraviolet radiation in cultures lacking the applicable scientific background, and for a culture which has not yet discovered gas as an entity, a cup full of hydrogen gas is apparently "empty." Here, we would have to take existing concepts like "light" or "breath" and create the more specialized concepts of "invisible light" (ultraviolet light is invisible) or "fiery breath" (hydrogen gas reacts with oxygen).

> **Idea**
>
> While different languages can make expressing ideas more or less difficult, no (complete) language can *prevent* you from expressing a certain idea at all.

Also, if we compare complete and consistent languages, the Sapir-Whorf hypothesis apparently does not apply. To be sure, a consistent language is less powerful; in contrast, in a translation from a complete language into a consistent one, we are dealing with *a concrete* fact, for which we also define new terms, if necessary, and expand the language. The same holds true in reverse; the complete language can indeed describe incorrect facts, but since it is complete, it can also describe the correct case in particular. So there are at most quantitative differences. A language which provides a greater spectrum of names for colors helps us to remember color perceptions for later.[29] A larger vocabulary serves as a mnemonic device for our memory and our mind to categorize information. If we translated the name of a color into a language with a less expressive color range, we might not be able to capture the measurement with the same accuracy.

We have now resolved the questions of communication concerning ourselves, our own knowledge, and culture. Proceeding a step further, in the following section, we confront the question of whether and how we can communicate with other forms of intelligence that might possess different sense organs (or "sensors") and "nervous systems" such as animals, extraterrestrial life forms, or computers.

### 2.3.3.4 Other Forms of Intelligence

**Question**

Without a common language, how could we communicate with one another? What would be the limitations involved?

The question of whether and how we could communicate with other forms of intelligence is not merely a question of the modern era or of science fiction. Over the course of their biological and cultural evolution, humans repeatedly have been confronted with other forms of intelligence. We came into contact with other tribes during the Stone Age, negotiated with Neanderthals, and cultivated relationships with animals (particularly wolves and subsequently dogs). In

---

[29] cf. Zimmer, *So kommt der Mensch zur Sprache*, pp. 196–97.

the modern era, we added apes, computers, and extraterrestrials[30] to the list, and we are only now beginning to communicate with whales, elephants, and dolphins. Especially with elephants and dolphins, scientists discovered a highly evolved form of social intelligence: elephants and dolphins grieve about deceased relatives, whales "sing," and dolphins take turns using "words" when communicating with each other.[31]

But what is the prerequisite for communication? We have described a so-called one-way communication, i.e., we simply express the image of our thoughts by a systematic vocalization. If we want to communicate with other intelligent beings, a two-way communication is required—our conversation partner has to be able to translate the image (our vocalization) back into concepts and respond accordingly. That requires that both conversation partners have a similar view of the world. For example, if we notice a fire, shouting "Fire!" might not be enough. Yes, we correctly identified the threat and translated the idea correctly into a proper statement. But we might still not be communicating with others if they do not share our language or if they use the word "fire" with a different meaning.

Somewhat more abstractly conceived, in the formulation of our thoughts, we do nothing other than encoding them using known definitions. Each of our words symbolically stands for an extensive body of knowledge, and behind each word, there may be a long chain of dependencies and definitions. With the use of a term such as "perception," we assume that our counterpart knows its definition, as well as the definitions of concepts like "property," "identity," "sensor," etc.

How do we now proceed with two-way communication if we cannot refer back to a common basis of terms? How do we speak, for

---

[30]At least theoretically and using a one-sided form of communication like the Arecibo message, see Figure 2.9.

[31]Ryabov, *The study of acoustic signals and the supposed spoken language of the dolphins.*

instance, with a dolphin, which lives in a completely different environment?

The idea is that we attempt to establish a common basis for our definitions. We can best achieve this through common experiences. At its core, a definition is the direct or indirect coupling of a word with reality. We show the dolphin a rubber ring and sound a tone intelligible to the dolphin (noun: "rubber ring"). We throw the ring and sound another tone (verb: "throw" or "fly"). Dolphins even possess the capability to correctly interpret pointing to objects without previously having been taught the signal. Even somewhat more complex commands which involve a number of objects (e.g., "Bring the toy to the bucket") can be communicated to and understood by a dolphin in this way. We can also observe this type of understanding of another person's intention in the development of children. The older the child becomes, the more far-reaching his understanding becomes, as well as the capability to conceptually couple remote objects with one another.[32] Step by step, we can convey current observations of the properties of entities (nouns), changes in properties (verbs), modes of change in properties (adverbs), etc., all through some form of demonstration. Depending on the capabilities of the conversation participants, we can thus talk with each other "completely normally."

---

**Idea**

If we are to communicate with another intelligent being, fundamentally we need to find a common language or build one from the ground up; the simplest possibility would be to pinch our counterpart on the arm, to point to the thing to which we are referring, and call out the name of its concept.

---

[32] cf. White, *In Defense of Dolphins: The New Moral Frontier*, pp. 68–74.

**Question**

Can we show that we can communicate with other intelligent beings and that merely technical barriers, time, and limited language capabilities stand in the way? Could other beings ever *really* understand what we mean?

Suppose our counterpart, due to eyes constructed differently than ours, sees red as green and vice versa. In a conversation, we get into a heated argument about the color of a flower, in which each of us believes to be seeing the "correct" color. An issue such as this is readily invoked by opponents of the assumption that objective communication is possible. How can we suppose that every person possesses the same structure in his or her head for comprehending colors, shapes, or abstractions? Depending on the individual brain, different types of information are stored in different brain regions which differ from person to person,[33] so how can we meet on the same level at all?

The image which we form from our thoughts and communicate with our counterpart can be perceived by her, so long as we have a common channel of communication (e.g., sound waves, light for symbols or text, cables for telecommunication, etc.). Ideally we learn all terms commonly, e.g., we pinch another person on the arm and point to a tree. We might possibly have entirely different brain structures and sense organs, but as long as we both perceive the same object or share the same situation, using our individual qualia (the conscious experiences of our perceptions) we can learn definitions that, although different, point to the same concepts.

Our definitions can be different because we recognize or understand only a part of the underlying concept. But we can amend them without contradiction (because we both refer to reality) by communicat-

---

[33] cf. Calvin and Ojemann, *Einsicht ins Gehirn: Wie Denken und Sprache entstehen*, pp. 224–30.

ing with the other person. For example, a dog could help us searching for a missing person. We both share the common concept of a person, but we identify someone by different means. Instead of showing the dog a picture, we give the dog a piece of clothing of the person. A deaf-blind person might categorize a dog by the fur and body shape while seeing persons focus on appearance. They have different qualia of the same thing, yet can identify and communicate it correctly once they have learned the common term. So, communication over our sensory and mental boundaries is possible if we learned the concept together.

It is important to note, of course, that this formation of concepts does not take place automatically. If we develop the wrong concepts, i.e., if we abstract incorrectly, then we may form contradicting definitions of the concept. But if we make no mistakes, we are inherently able to form *correct* definitions. If this were not possible, we could not argue against it (fallacy of the stolen concept). Argumentation requires the objectivity of communication. If we argue *against* the objectivity of communication, we contradict ourselves by our very actions.

So, even if our sense organs and brains are built completely differently, we can conclude that in principle, we are able to communicate with all concept-forming beings, presumably including computers. In the example of red/green-vision, we would simply point to a tree. We couple the spoken word "tree" with "green" and with the qualia (our image of the tree). Regardless of the differences in our sense organs, we both could have the same understanding of the appearance of a tree despite our different qualia. Even if our individual qualia of green objects are ultimately different, we still create similar qualia for all green objects.

Even more obvious is the aforementioned Pirahã language, wherein there is no term for color, but simply comparisons or relations, e.g., "a color like blood" or "a color like grass." Objective communication can be built in this way. Essentially, the point is that colors are *measurements* and not fundamental properties of an object since there is no property of "green-ness" inherent in plants. Instead, the reflected light can be gradually measured and categorized, but the formation of a concept of a "green entity" in this way would be pointless.

But *what* should we speak about with other intelligent beings? There may be no common reference; they may perceive plants, animals, air, water, fire, and the heavens quite differently. To start with, we say that concept-forming beings possess the capability of abstraction; for instance, even if these intelligent beings were to perceive the sun only through fluctuations in the ultraviolet region of light, we could group these fluctuations with our own term "visible light" under a common meaning. The measurement would be different, the definitions would be the same.

But what if there is absolutely no common ground for communication? What if the other intelligent being is so different that that being possesses no sense organs (or at least not the same type as ours)? We could imagine a supercomputer buried deep in the Earth, connected only by a cable to the external world. Can we "speak" to this computer? Yes, if only to a limited extent. Essentially, this computer *does* possess "sense organs," namely sensors which interpret electrical signals which someone from the surface provides. The common basis of communication would be everything related to these signals; particularly this would be physical and mathematical formulas and problems. Of course we could convey only with difficulty how, for example, it feels to walk barefoot through damp grass on a sunny spring morning, just as the computer conversely would have difficulty explaining to us what a memory overflow "feels like." The only common points of reference about which we could converse would be electrical currents or information theory. The question also arises whether this computer can possess self-awareness at all if it has no actuators at its disposal with which it can influence—and thus literally experience and grasp—the world and, therefore, itself.

In popular culture, a depiction of computers communicating can be found in *Colossus: The Forbin Project,* in which two computers of different construction have developed a common language for higher concepts using commonalities in logical terms. Despite what the film portrays, the mere exchange of mathematical regularities as the basis of such communication would *not* suffice. A simple transmission of a series of prime numbers could be quickly filtered out of the noise of other protocol information and decoded by the receiver. But if both computer systems otherwise possess no common knowledge about elements of reality, then the communication remains on the level of the common ground of communication: *data.* Mathematicians could exchange views this way, but for a communication about more complex concepts, both would have to possess knowledge of, e.g., physics, and world maps, but above all about self-reflection, their own mortality, their own "construction plan," morality, values, history, philosophy, and so on.

Keeping that in mind, what would the solution for both aforementioned computers look like? They could map each other's sensory information and existing data of the real world in the form of geographical coordinates of certain cities or satellite pictures. But what the computers cannot do, and indeed no one can, is to take a basic insight such as $A = A$ and then follow truths about the world with no empirical knowledge about the world.

## 2.3.3.5 The Arecibo Message

> **Question**
>
> If two parties had only one thing in common in terms of communication, what would it be?

While we have not had contact with extraterrestrials so far, we can still assume they exist and send radio messages into space. When communicating with them, we can presume at the outset that they have dealt with similar concepts in a common reality. If both parties built signal stations pointing into space, they certainly have a lot to talk about. NASA designed a message in the 1970s, the so-called "Arecibo message" (see Figure 2.9). It served as a study in the requirements of formulating communication with alien intelligence. It was transmitted in 1974 in binary format over radio waves in the direction of a cluster of stars 22,800 light-years away.

The message begins with a binary encoding of the numbers 1 to 10, logical components for understanding the remainder of the message. Following that is a list of the atomic numbers of biochemical elements essential to life: 1: hydrogen (H), 6: carbon (C), 7: nitrogen (N), 8: oxygen (O), and 15: phosphorus (P). This encoding then is used to represent the molecules of which our DNA is composed. The four elements on the left and right represent the structural component of the double-strand DNA, while the four elements in the center represent the four letters (A, T, C, G) which encode our genetic information. For example, adenine (C5H4N5) consists of four hydrogen atoms, five carbon atoms, five nitrogen atoms, zero oxygen and zero phosphorus atoms. In the next section follows the spatial configuration of the DNA as a double helix, as well as the estimated number of DNA base pairs possessed by humans—again binary encoded. All of this information conveys the complexity of

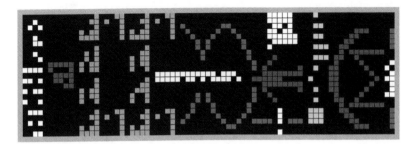

**Figure 2.9:** Arecibo message

the human organism. In the next section, besides a binary representation of the human population on Earth, the shape and physical size of a human is represented—a considerable challenge in communication with an alien life form, as we have no common gauge at our disposal. In which unit of measurement should we convey a dimension like length? Absent the commonly held experiences mentioned earlier, only the communication channel itself remains since both sides know the wavelength of the message. After a representation of the solar system with an emphasis on the Earth, there follows lastly a graphic illustration and diameter of the Arecibo radio telescope transmitting the message. Again, the wavelength was used as the only available gauge of measurement as a reference to define its diameter.

---

**Idea**

If we share no common basis for communication with our counterpart, the communication channel itself can be utilized as a basis. In the case of the Arecibo message, scientists used the wavelength of the signal as a reference point.

The special format of the message was chosen so that we could both convey information and make it easier for a potential observer to detect the signal amid the ambient radiation. Here, we must consider the fact that we believed we had already detected evidence of extraterrestrial intelligence, due to radio signals. In 1968, we discovered a regular, rapidly repeating, and highly precise radio signal emanating from a star system. But after further research, it was discovered to be a neutron star which produced the signal by its high rotation speed. In the universe, some things look artificially created but are instead the result of repeated complex processes.

An interesting consequence of all these considerations is that it could be possible to write a "perfect book." That is, a book which in principle any person could understand completely, even without any background knowledge. It would provide, in one heavily illustrated chapter, an introduction to the language, an explanation of grammar and verbs, and then—like this book—lead into a discussion of the objectivity of language and philosophy. Beyond that, how "expressive" such a book could be naturally depends on the extent of commonly held experiences between the author and readers.

Like the radio waves of the Arecibo message, a book held in the hand offers at least a small indication of a common reality: the author creates with it a common point of reference with the reader, a type of common universe to which he can refer. A comparison like "as large as the printed version of this book" gives the reader a clear standard of measurement, and printed illustrations provide visual mappings of the real world.

### 2.3.3.6 Trust

**Question**

How can you establish trust in communication?

Even if we share our definitions and concept hierarchy, and even if we are aware of cultural and translation issues, communication could still be impeded: our counterpart's sense perception could be distorted by hallucinogenic drugs, psychiatric illness, optical illusions, etc., or he could simply be not willing to tell us the truth. If we talk to our future selves, for example by keeping a journal, then we can trust ourselves. Without further stipulations, however, communication with *others* is dubious. While we indeed can examine our counterpart's mental condition by investing a lot of effort, it remains unsettled whether a statement made by our counterpart represents the truth—we simply must trust him.

We can establish this trust by ensuring that our counterpart has a stake in truthful communication, whether due to selflessness or long-term-oriented thinking. Such a condition would occur if we could either assume that we would be able to contact this person again in the future (and in some way punish them for lying or show our appreciation for their honesty), or if there were an institution functioning to detect lies, enforce the truth, and publicize the honesty (or lack thereof) of each person (possibly done by the government through contract law, a community of reputable truth-lovers, or by a private verification organization like the Better Business Bureau).

> **Idea**
>
> You can establish trust in conversation by ensuring that a participant can benefit from telling the truth and must face consequences when lying.

Similar to scientific experiments, wherein we must keep an eye on the test conditions and limitations, such knowledge obtained through communication always depends on our confidence in the source. Were we to find out later that our counterpart lied to us, was hallucinating, used different concepts, or himself fell victim to a lie, we may once again have to reevaluate all knowledge gained from this source and knowledge we derived from that knowledge. Without an institution or system that allows us to trust the word of others, we would have to rely (like the aforementioned Pirahã tribe) on a purely empirical language and provide explicit sources instead of relying on hearsay.

> **Did you know?**
>
> The reason both proper citations and copyright are so crucial to knowledge management and accountability of the author is that they create the trust necessary for objective communication. The most successful trust network is the scientific community. It allows you to use and trust the results of anyone involved.
>
> $\longrightarrow$ Read more in *Philosophy for Heroes: Continuum*

### 2.3.3.7 Language in Society

> [O]ne should imagine thirty or more hominids gathered together: males, females, and infants; those of high status and those of low status; individuals with different personalities and emotions; those with resources to share and those wishing to consume some food. Emanating from the site would have been a variety of calls, reflecting the diversity of activities, how these changed through the day, and the varying emotional states of individuals and the group as a whole. One might have heard predator alarm calls; calls relating to food availability and requests for help with butchery; mother-infant communications; the sounds of pairs and small groups maintaining their social bonds by communicating with melodic calls; and the vocalizations of individuals expressing particular emotions and seeking to induce them in others. Finally, at dusk, one should perhaps imagine synchronized vocalizations—a communal song—that induced calm emotions in all individuals and faded away into silence as night fell and the hominids went to sleep in the trees.

—Steven Mithen, *The Singing Neanderthals—the Origins of Music, Language, Mind, and Body*

Without this "proto-language"—music or singing respectively—our ancestors would never have been able to get together in large hunting groups. As individuals, we are different and complex. Without means to find common ground with music or direct communication, we could never have solved our inner and outer conflicts peacefully. In smaller groups, apes prove that bonding without language is possible, after all. They practice mutual grooming as a sign of friendship. The time needed for grooming serves as a common investment in the connection between the two individuals. Although apes do have the ability for vocal expression, they do not have the ability to focus this "language" in the same way that they can with grooming a single individual. Without a theory of mind, they cannot value the individual experiences you could chat about. We, on the other hand, have in a way replaced our fur with our eardrums, in that we foster our friendships by telling stories and singing together while we have our hands free for our everyday work.

Our distant ancestors did not have means to expand their knowledge as a group. Of course, they could learn from and experience the world on an individual basis; but without a possibility to preserve knowledge (aside from skills that can be demonstrated directly) for the next generation, every generation had to start at the beginning and literally reinvent the wheel again and again. While you can certainly use existing wheels as a model, the techniques for creating one requires a teacher with a theory of mind.

When we reached the threshold of a higher order of intentionality and then were able, for the first time, to amass knowledge by communicating words—first orally and then later in writing—there was an explosive growth of what each generation was able to learn. Every new generation was able to acquire their insights on top of the insights of the previous generation and very soon, humanity had access to thousands of years of the mental capacity of others. Concerning our biological evolution, we are at the very edge between the possibility to just amass knowledge on our own and the ability to acquire the knowledge of others. It took a long time until we were physiologically able to communicate in a reasonable fashion. But as soon as this level was reached, our horizon expanded multifold within a very short span of time.

The invention of language has exponentially increased the intellectual possibilities of humankind. Only thoughts conceived in language are communicable and can be stored; all others decay after a few seconds. Thus, language helps us in thinking—by concretizing, specifying, fixating, and stabilizing the presumably simultaneous swirling and bubbling of our manifold intertwined concepts; by sharpening them into usable terms; and by organizing combinations of these concepts with grammar.[34]

**Question**

What makes communication beneficial, and why?

Each person holds a monopoly on his individual experiences so that the more individualistic the society, the more we profit from two-way communication. The Internet immediately provides a quick glance into this resource of global exchange. It is comparable maybe with the former Apple CEO Steve Jobs' famous quote relating to how computers have empowered our minds in the modern world:

> I think one of the things that really separates us from the high primates is that we're tool builders. I read a study that measured the efficiency of locomotion for various species on the planet. The condor used the least energy to move a kilometer. And, humans came in with a rather unimpressive showing, about a third of the way down the list. It was not too proud a showing for the crown of creation. So, that didn't look so good. But, then somebody at *Scientific American* had the insight to test the efficiency of locomotion for a man on a bicycle. And, a man on a bicycle, a human on a bicycle, blew the condor away, completely off the top of the charts. And that's what a computer is to me. What a computer is to me is it's the most remarkable tool that we've ever come up with, and it's the equivalent of a bicycle for our minds.

—Steve Jobs, *Memory and Imagination*

---

[34]cf. Zimmer, *So kommt der Mensch zur Sprache*, p. 205.

> **Idea**
>
> Only our very individual experiences make communication useful. The more similar we become to each other (in terms of our individual experiences), the more shallow our conversations can become, with less new information being shared.

We are all different and everyone has a unique story to tell. We interpret language differently and that is why in conversations, we should always try to first find a common ground. This openness towards others is what opens our soul to a fruitful discussion. This is the second building block on your path from a student of philosophy to a teacher and ultimately a leader.

# The Book Series
## *Philosophy for Heroes*

" But the true secret of being a hero lies in knowing the order of things. The swineherd cannot already be wed to the princess when he embarks on his adventures, nor can the boy knock at the witch's door when she is away on vacation. The wicked uncle cannot be found out and foiled before he does something wicked. Things must happen when it is time for them to happen. Quests may not simply be abandoned; prophecies may not be left to rot like unpicked fruit; unicorns may go unrescued for a long time, but not forever. The happy ending cannot come in the middle of the story.

—Peter S. Beagle, *The Last Unicorn*

$\text{T}$HE BOOK SERIES continues! Head over to our shop for more from this series (soon): https://www.lode.de/shop.

**Part I: Knowledge.** In *Philosophy for Heroes: Knowledge*, the first book in a four-book series, author Clemens Lode takes the reader on a journey, examining the foundations of knowledge. What is the basis of our understanding of the world? How does society define a "hero"? How do basic skills, such as language and mathematics, train our way of thinking and reasoning?

**Part II: Continuum.** Beyond the static world of the first book, *Philosophy for Heroes: Continuum* looks at gradual transitions from one condition to the next. Where do we come from? Why is there something rather than nothing? What is the source of our creativity? How can the study of natural sciences help us to understand who we are?

**Part III: Act.** Being a hero requires not only courage and knowledge, but also independence and consistency. *Philosophy for Heroes: Act* sets the reader's mind free from harmful manipulation by others. How can the fields of ethics and psychology help us to discover our true self, our true potential? What "masks" do people wear unknowingly? What are illusionary values? What is the meaning of life? How do we embody our values? What are the challenges we face when being independent?

**Part IV: Epos.** The final book in the series, *Philosophy for Heroes: Epos*, examines the influence of the most powerful tool of a leader, the *story*. Is the age-old conflict between "good" and "evil" necessary? Do heroes need "dragons"? What can we learn from the ancient stories of religion? How can we use our language for good? How can our own life become a story, an *epos*?

# The Creation of this Book Series

 The only good teachers for you are those friends who love you, who think you are interesting, or very important, or wonderfully funny; whose attitude is: "Tell me more. Tell me all you can. I want to understand more about everything you feel and know and all the changes inside and out of you. Let more come out." And if you have no such friend—and you want to write—well, then you must imagine one.

—Brenda Ueland, *If You Want to Write: A Book about Art, Independence and Spirit*

Dear reader, the book you hold in your hands is the product of my research and contemplation over the past fifteen years. The idea for this book was born out of the notes of many discussions I had and books I read. All the participants and authors have my gratitude for their opinions and input, as well as for the opportunity they gave me to reflect on my own ideas. I would like to thank especially the readers of the early drafts, and my editor for the English publication; all went above and beyond to help make the book a reality.

Now, allow me to tell you a little about its childhood. Like a stranger on the street, the book would like to introduce itself and shake your hand. One does not start a book by sitting in front of a blank sheet of paper and writing down the first sentence. This book series existed for a long time in my head and then on many small pieces of paper. The actual *writing* of a book consists of connecting and arranging ideas together to create a coherent whole. Over the course of five years, I researched, digitized, and edited my notes. And out of all these *tesserae*, a picture emerged—the theme of this book series, a *Philosophy for Heroes*.

# 1 Conception

> [...] the dark future which never came still exists for me. And it always will, like the traces of a dream. [...] [But] if a machine can learn the value of human life, maybe we can, too.
>
> —*Terminator 2: Judgment Day*

In its infacy, this book was but a jumble of ideas with me as its companion. If I had to pinpoint its actual beginning, it would likely be 20 years ago, reading Dawkins' book *The Selfish Gene*. I devoured it during my time in school and, with its help, I began to grasp some of the connections in the world. We all craft for ourselves a model of the world, although at the time, human motivations were incomprehensible to me. That book provided me with my first model, with which I could at least begin to examine people's behavior. My interest in mathematics and computers supplemented this, allowing me to actually simulate models.

During my final years at school, I developed a computer program to calculate optimal business processes and workflows using algorithms based on nature and depicted them graphically. For the first time, I felt that I was coming close to understanding the driving force that keeps the world together and explains its nature. Eventually, I began studying computer science in Karlsruhe, Germany, and took a number of advanced courses. I continued to develop my program and conducted research for several years in the field of artificial evolution, which ultimately led to my specialization in operations research. In this field, the big question is: How can we achieve the maximum result using limited resources? Here again, the focus was on nature and its inherent harmony: a chaotic system which, from the outside, appears to be in balance.

In terms of my career, I was at a crossroads. Should I pursue these abstract systems more deeply or should I focus on the university's area of expertise, robotics? At that time, influenced by a certain prevalent "anti-technology" atmosphere, and some "doom-sayers" speaking pessimistically about the future of humanity, I decided against it and for the study of algorithms in nature. While I found robotics interesting, I could not see myself creating "beings" for others to control.

## 2 Aporia

> The people who came to see Socrates usually thought that they knew what they were talking about, but after half an hour of his relentless questioning, they discovered that they knew nothing at all about such basic issues as justice or courage. They felt deeply perplexed, like bewildered children; the intellectual and moral foundations of their lives had been radically undermined, and they experienced a frightening, vertiginous doubt (*aporia*). For Socrates, that was the moment when a person became a philosopher, a "lover of wisdom," because he had become aware that he longed for greater insight, knew he did not have it, but would henceforth seek it as ardently as a lover pursues his beloved. Thus dialogue led participants not to certainty but to a shocking realization of the profundity of human ignorance. However carefully, logically, and rationally Socrates and his friends analyzed it, something always eluded them. Yet many found that the initial shock of *aporia* led to *ekstatsis* because they had "stepped outside" their former selves.

—Karen Armstrong, *Twelve Steps to a Compassionate Life*

T HE FEAR I had as an eight-year-old when the Gulf War began is still in my memory. But I did not consciously perceive world events as such and I did not feel connected to the world as a whole before the (second) Iraq War. Not because I was directly affected or had a political opinion about it, but because I was unable to comprehend its context and the reasons for it. This was not the first event in my life that caused me to think beyond my horizons, but it certainly marked the point at which I began to question my viewpoints and to see myself as part of a larger community. Maybe this "shock" (*aporia*) was what people felt when encountering and discussing with

Socrates in ancient Greece the concept that life no longer revolved around the here and now, but instead, revolved around history, the future, and one's own role in it.

In the following months and years, I began studying history, law, economics, and politics with renewed interest. I reflected on my historical self, i.e., the "mask" we are each made to wear by school, culture, history, and the media. I learned about crime and corruption; but despite all my research, unanswered questions remained. Is it only the greed and the lust for power that run the world? Are there a few secret powers turning the wheel of history? Which side can be trusted? I grappled with these questions during many sleepless nights. Certainly, there are company mergers, various interest groups, and organizations. There are the mafia and the international drug trade. There are corruption and political intrigue. But do these systems operate independently from human action, and are we powerless against them? Is it sufficient to identify them in order to defeat them? Is it enough to know the names of people in key positions? How could such an extensive or powerful network operate on the basis of violence?

Eventually, it was Ayn Rand who provided an answer in *The Virtue of Selfishness* and *Capitalism: The Unknown Ideal*. Politics is the product of the philosophy of a society. No matter what sort of evil intentions an individual might have, he cannot easily make others do his bidding. We each have free will. We have values and imagination. Only if these are corrupted, a human becomes a slave to a manipulator.[1] Instead of arguing in the political realm, it is more fruitful to contemplate our values and discuss them with others.

---

[1] Being manipulated by others, in itself, is not necessarily a bad thing. For example, we might hire a motivational trainer that uses persuasion techniques to get us to eat healthily and exercise regularly, and to push us to our limits.

From this starting point, I was able to distance myself from superficial political debates and actually name real causes. It became clear to me that many misunderstandings and conflicts of opinion have their origins at a far deeper level than it would appear. Apart from being influenced by peer pressure, no one is automatically part of a particular political party; only a complete series of opinions, including those involving very abstract themes, leads to these convictions. With my new insights into philosophy, I was able to see connections between different disciplines of thought. From hard logic and fundamental philosophy, to questions about cognition, to questions about one's way of life, politics, and esthetics, I could finally consider the world in a unified vision. And I thought back to a book I read in my childhood—Peter S. Beagle's *The Last Unicorn*, which was very much like what Joseph Campbell described in *The Hero with a Thousand Faces*: a hero's journey, the development of a human being toward the realization of what is truly important to him. We are not always what we appear to be; we wear "masks" while we are on a search for our values, our true nature.

Having acquired this knowledge, not only did I begin to understand the world, but also to understand myself. I was finally able to access my true self. Now, the next step is to teach others. Because, like joy, knowledge only becomes truly valuable when shared with others. My driving force is seeing the unrealized potential in myself as well as in the people of the world. I feel that each of us can become a better person and that we are only missing the impulse and the knowledge to do so. With books like this one, I want to convey a small portion of this impulse and knowledge.

# 3  Becoming a Teacher

From studying psychology, especially the work of Carl Jung, I started to realize the difficulty of sharing this knowledge with others. Everyone constructs a certain personality-type theory based on characteristics such as female, male, introverted, extroverted, intelligent, etc. We know, of course, that all people are different. But Carl Jung's work in psychoanalysis has shown me that people can have *substantially* different ways of thinking, and correspondingly different personalities. In this book series, I try to accommodate all personality types. In the end, however, I am writing from my own point of view, reflecting my own mode of thinking and my own values.

Researching this book series, I took a deep interest in many views about life, and subsequently questioned my own views. If you want to really study other ideas, you have to "feel" yourself into them. And you have to let down your guard. That is the cost of dealing with other people: you must leave your safe garden. While it is easy to refer to other teachers and other literature, the process of teaching something you have mastered yourself takes courage.

Who am I to tell you what to do, especially when my philosophy is about freedom of the mind? I often ask myself if I am *truly* right. But then again, there are others who, for their own gain, manipulate people and tell them what to do, so the world needs a counter-balance which can free people. But this, of course, is a story I prepared for myself as a justification. I think the main idea a teacher must internalize is that he should not try to protect his students from making mistakes. That is more a job for a consultant whom you hire to manage part of your life.

A good teacher has to go beyond just teaching the conclusions and instead enable others to discover something for themselves. Some things can easily be *known* in advance but only *learned* when facing a specific situation and experiencing what happens if you do *not* follow the advice. A teacher should be more like an open book, answering questions and providing ever more difficult challenges in the face of which the pupil can grow and discover his own limits.

A teacher cultivates leaders, not followers. It is up to each person what he will do with his freedom of mind. As teachers, rather than tell people what they should do, we can give them the freedom to be themselves.

# The Author

" If you give me the right man in any field I can talk to him. I know what the condition is: That he did whatever he did as far as he can go. That he studied every aspect of it as far as he has stretched himself to the end. He is not a dilletant in any way. [...] And, therefore, he is up against mysteries all the way around the end. And awe. Mystery and awe, that's what we have in common.

—Richard Feynman

What would lead a computer scientist to turn to philosophy for answers? Clemens Lode has a passion for solving problems by applying nature-inspired algorithms. In his examination into what makes computers "smart," he found that the answer requires more than just science...

Clemens Lode is the founder LODE Publishing, established to create a blueprint for heroes. His goal is to do this by providing a foundation in classical philosophy and modern science. His dream is to create a better world by teaching people what it means to be a hero —and how to become a hero in real life.

Clemens received his Masters in computer science from the Karlsruhe Institute of Technology. After focusing his studies on nature-inspired optimization, and his professional career on large-scale health-care server applications, he moved on to optimizing businesses and, ultimately, helping improve individual lives. Before creating LODE Publishing, he founded a company dedicated to bringing the power of nature to computers. Its most successful product was a program that used evolutionary algorithms to optimize game strategies—a task Google recently took up for its development of artificial intelligence. Clemens currently works as a business IT consultant, analyzing organization structure, team psychology, and helping with IT processes.

He would love to hear from you, drop him a line, or follow him on Facebook or Twitter! Besides an occasional commentary on politics, his feed is usually filled with cute animal pictures. For him, they represent innocence, opportunities, a fresh start, a positive attitude about life, and curiosity. Clemens can be reached via Twitter @ClemensLode, Facebook, or email (clemens@lode.de).

# Reflection

Dɪᴅ ʏᴏᴜ ꜰɪɴᴅ all the *Kami no Itte*? Join the vibrant conversation with other readers in our online forum at: https://www.lode.de/study/pfh1

## Knowledge

- How is wishing to be in the spotlight on television similar to a *cargo cult*?

- Why should we not study philosophy as passive observers?

- What are false heroes, and how does a true hero interact with them?

- Why can science not answer fundamental philosophical questions?

- Why is it important to study philosophy as a participant in the world and not just as a passive observer?

- Can contradictions exist in reality if we can imagine them?

- What is the nature of the identity of an entity?

- Why are ontology and epistemology simultaneous?

- Which five issues could have a detrimental effect on our objective perception?

- What, if any, effect on us must remain hidden?

- How should we deal with arbitrary claims?

- Why is it necessary for concepts to be based upon observations, but not measurements?

- How do concepts increase our mental capacity?

- Definitions do not need to be complete; what is their role?

- How are contradictions in statements related to concepts?

- To what concept does a magenta ball belong—to the concept of the blue or the red balls?

- How do humans and computers compare in terms of comprehending an actual issue?

- How does the process of deduction supplement the process of induction?

- Are we spirits who discovered their bodies, or the other way around?

- How would the concept of "concept" lose its meaning in extreme empiricism?

- Can statements be shown to be true without induction? Why or why not?

- What does Hume's problem of induction have to do with omniscience?

# Language

- How did ancient sea-trading affect the development of our current alphabet?

- What is an example of a consistent language? What is an example of a complete one?

- Aside from concept hierarchy, what makes languages complex?

- How do children learn the concepts "past" and "future"?

- What is an example of a fourth order of intentionality?

- What are the three most significant obstacles in our communication with others?

- What is the importance of corresponding definitions in a discussion?

- How do languages differ in terms of expressiveness?

- Why can no (complete) language prevent you from expressing a certain idea?

- Why did humankind develop a system of mathematics?

- Sets are not, themselves, entities; what are they?

- Why can sets not contain themselves?

- Why is it that axiomatic systems in mathematics need not have a connection to reality?

- What are possible shortcomings of a recursive description of natural numbers?

- Why is mathematics not simply a science of entities?

- If the circle circumference is "irrational," does this mean that there are no circles in reality? How do irrational numbers appear in nature?

- What aspect of nature is the source of its complexity?

- What is the relationship between counting and philosophy?

- Does "zero" have an equivalent in reality? If you have "zero" apples and "zero" lemons, is what you have (in terms of apples and lemons) the same?

- What are some of the limits of mathematics in terms of describing reality?

- Can we show that we can communicate with other intelligent beings and that merely technical barriers, time, and limited language capabilities stand in the way? Could other beings ever *really* understand what we mean?

- Without a common language, how could we communicate with one another? What would be the limitations involved?

- If two parties had only one thing in common in terms of communication, what would it be?

- How can you establish trust in communication?

- What makes communication beneficial, and why?

# Kami no Itte

THE IDEA BOXES which you can find throughout the book do not cover all the contents of the book, but they are cornerstones within which the philosophy is placed. Like the 神の 一手—*Kami no Itte*—mentioned at the beginning of the book, they are unique, sometimes surprising "moves" (ideas) from which deeper insights can be extracted.

## Knowledge

- The opposite of a hero is not his opponent but, instead, the passive observer.

- A true hero stands up to false heroes.

- Science is built upon a philosophical foundation, and thus is a branch of philosophy. Science cannot answer fundamental philosophical questions without violating its own scientific principles.

- The essence of philosophy is to understand yourself as being part of reality, rather than isolating yourself from reality as a passive observer.

- Entities have exactly one (specific and distinct) identity at any given time.

- Ontology and epistemology are simultaneous—what exists and how we know it form a foundation of philosophy.

- We can overcome physical limitations of our senses through the use of our minds and scientific instruments. No effect on us necessarily needs to remain hidden.

- Arbitrary claims can be ignored. Just because you can make the claim does not mean that it has any connection to reality that needs to be considered.

- Concepts are generated through the omission of measurements.

- With the aid of concepts, we can make statements about the behavior of a large number of entities without having to consider them individually. This way, we increase our mental capacities multifold.

- Definitions do not need to be complete; they simply must be able to clearly separate concepts from one another.

- The origin of contradictions lies either in the faulty definition of concepts or in the faulty allocation of entities to concepts.

- A computer is like a large stack of indexed file cards in which a programmer can represent a concept hierarchy similar to our own in a structured way. Both computers and humans use concept hierarchies to categorize elements of a situation.

- We are not spirits that deduce from their consciousness that they also must possess bodies. We are also not bodies who have learned to perceive the world and form a consciousness. We are both at the same time and we need to discover both at the same time.

• In extreme empiricism, the concept hierarchy tree would be completely flat and the concept of "concepts" would lose its meaning, because every concept would correspond only to one single instance.

• By the Axiom of Identity, Kant's synthetic *a priori* statements cannot exist. That means that there are no statements that can be shown to be true without induction. Kant's examination does not solve the problem of induction.

• Hume's problem of induction is ultimately directed at the fact that we are not omniscient when we establish concepts.

# Language

• Our present-day writing system descends from the Phoenician alphabet. It was a writing system that emerged in the ancient Mediterranean sea-trading environment and that depicted sounds used in speech (phonemes) instead of pictorial representations of concepts.

• Each (sufficiently powerful) formal system is either inconsistent or incomplete (Gödel's First Incompleteness Theorem).

• Concept hierarchy aside, languages are basically trivial. Only including optimizations like time-related changes and pronouns makes them complex.

• Before we run hot-headed into a discussion about, e.g., God, democracy, equality, or freedom, we must ask our discussion partner for the corresponding definitions.

• Differences between languages regarding their expressiveness concern only the length, accuracy, and clarity of their sentences.

• While different languages can make expressing ideas more or less difficult, no (complete) language can *prevent* you from expressing a certain idea at all.

• Mathematics arose from the need to count quantities, to compare quantities, and to describe processes.

• Sets are only *enumerations* of existing entities or other sets, not the entities themselves.

• Sets have to be countable and cannot contain themselves.

• Axiomatic systems in mathematics need not have a connection to reality or be self-evident. They are purely rationalistic, self-contained systems.

• The recursive description of natural numbers indeed supplies a complete picture of reality, but, unfortunately, it is a potentially erroneous picture.

• Mathematics is *not* the science of entities, but rather principally the science of *relations* of entities, that is to say, *measurements* of their properties.

• Irrational numbers do not refer to quantities or ratios and do not appear in nature as such. Instead, they refer to processes, or methods of generation (circles, golden ratio, leaf arrangements, proportions, etc.).

● The complexity of reality stems from the fact that it is a *product* of infinitely repeating processes.

● Counting is not a trivial capability or an innate one, but rather a deeply internalized expression of a system of philosophy learned early in life and embodied in language and culture.

● The *digit* "0" originally served merely as a blank space, while the *number* "0" has no identity and thus no equivalent in reality but can only represent the result of a measurement and is mostly used as a form of negation. You could count an infinite list of things that you own 0 items of, without ever making progress to describe *what* you own.

● Reality is without contradiction. Mathematics is a good *tool* to describe measurements of reality. But a "nice" mathematical model that reflects the results of measurements exactly still remains a *model* and is not necessarily a description of reality.

● If we are to communicate with another intelligent being, fundamentally we need to find a common language or build one from the ground up; the simplest possibility would be to pinch our counterpart on the arm, to point to the thing to which we are referring, and call out the name of its concept.

● If we share no common basis for communication with our counterpart, the communication channel itself can be utilized as a basis. In the case of the Arecibo message, scientists used the wavelength of the signal as a reference point.

● You can establish trust in conversation by ensuring that a participant can benefit from telling the truth and must face consequences when lying.

● Only our very individual experiences make communication useful. The more similar we become to each other (in terms of our individual experiences), the more shallow our conversations can become, with less new information being shared.

# Glossary

## A

***A posteriori* statement** • An *a posteriori statement* is a statement that must be substantiated through experience (for example, "bodies are heavy;" we must first lift a body to determine its weight).

***A priori* knowledge** • *A priori knowledge* is knowledge that was acquired without first engaging in an experience.

***A priori* statement** • An *a priori statement* is a statement that can be substantiated independently of experience (e.g., mathematical statements).

**Adjective** • An *adjective* is a word that describes a corresponding noun in more detail. It adds a measurement to a property of the corresponding concept (e.g., "a *tall* tree").

**Adverb** • An *adverb* is a word that refers to a verb and compares the mode or degree of change in properties with another change in properties (e.g., "She treaded down the hallway *quietly*"); alternatively, an adverb can relate to an adjective or another adverb and describe it more accurately (e.g., "He had *very* big eyes").

**Aggregate** • An *aggregate* is a number of entities that have a reciprocal effect on one another, so that they can be considered collectively as their own entity (e.g., a cup full of water—all water molecules interact with each other).

**Analytic statement** • An *analytic statement* is a statement whose assertion is given by the definition of the subject. As a result, measurements are not necessary to determine whether it is true or not (e.g., "Triangles have three vertices").

**Axiom** • An *axiom* is a self-evident truth (e.g., "Something exists").

**Axiom of consciousness** • The *axiom of consciousness* states that we can become aware of our existence, our identity, and the external world.

**Axiom of existence** • The *axiom of existence* states that something *exists*. Without existence, there would be no entities. Particularly, there would be no interactions between entities, no perception, and, for this reason, no knowledge; a line of reasoning for this axiom would not be possible.

**Axiom of identity** • The *axiom of identity* states that *something* exists. Without this axiom, "entities" could *possibly* exist, but they would have no identity and, for this reason, would likewise possess no properties. In such a reality, it follows that no perception or knowledge would be possible either; particularly, we could not form arguments against the axiom of identity: without identity, statements in general would be impossible because they, too, would have no identity —no statement. In Objectivism, this axiom is also designated as "*A* is *A*": every identity has *definite* properties and no others.

**Axiomatic system** • An *axiomatic system* is the set of axioms that is the foundation of all knowledge within a field of study.

## C

**Cargo cult** • A *cargo cult* refers to the behavior where someone tries to imitate certain aspects of another (successful) person, expecting the same success. For example, celebrities are often on TV but just by managing to get yourself on TV, you will not necessarily become a celebrity.

**Category** • A *category* is the mental correlation between entities.

**Causality** • *Causality* refers to the effect of one or several entities on another entity in a certain situation (e.g., an accident is no random occurrence, there are one or several causes which led to the accident, such as lack of sleep, a technical defect, poor visibility, etc.).

**Cause** • A *cause* refers to the entity that has or had an effect on another entity (e.g., the ice cube in the glass is the cause for the drink having gotten cold).

**Cognition** • *Cognition* is the faculty for processing and correcting qualia, generating and applying knowledge, changing preferences, as well as reflecting on the process of cognition itself. The result of the process of cognition is consciousness.

**Communication** • *Communication* is the attempt of an entity *A* to translate knowledge (whether real or invented) of a situation through language into images and linguistic auxiliary structures, so that another entity *B* can translate the series of images and linguistic auxiliary structures into knowledge of a situation perceived by *A*, without itself having obtained immediate sense data from the entities participating in the situation.

**Concept** • A *concept* is a category that is delineated by a definition, and determined by the nature of the entity.

**Concept hierarchy** • A *concept hi-*
*erarchy* is a tree-like structure consisting of concepts, defined by the definitions of given connections (e.g., "chair" and "table" are furniture, the concept "furniture" would thus constitute the root of a tree and "chair" and "table" are two successive branches).

**Conceptual common denominator** • If a concept inherits from more than one other concept, these additional concepts will be called *conceptual common denominators*. For example, we can classify a "human" entity into the concept "mammal" just as well as the concept "biped."

**Configuration of a property** • The *configuration of a property* relates to the intensity of a certain property of an entity.

**Consciousness** • With our *consciousness*, we can become conscious about something, therefore, it is the *process* that emerges from the faculty of an entity to reflect on and to perceive oneself and other entities and their properties (cognition).

**Contradiction** • A *contradiction* can result from a (possibly erroneous) logical integration. This becomes visible when the corresponding concept has a property while *not having* it at the same time (such as an invisible pink unicorn, boiling ice, a full empty cup, etc.).

# D

**Deduction** • With *deduction*, we conclude from the general case the special case. For this, we use the knowledge that we gained from induction, check if a certain perception fits the definition of a concept, and conclude for the corresponding entity that it has all the properties of the corresponding concept. In short, deduction is the process of subsuming new instances under a known concept (cf. Rand, Binswanger, and Peikoff, *Introduction to Objectivist Epistemology*, p. 28). Deduction thus operates in the opposite direction as induction. For example, if we notice that cars can drive on the street, and we see a parked car, then we can deduct that this car is able to drive on the street as well, because we have assigned the parked car to the known concept "car."

**Definition** • A *definition* is the possible demarcation of a number of entities by means of perceptions, concepts, and axioms (e.g., grass is a "plant," a "living organism" which uses "photosynthesis.") It consists of a list of properties and processes of entities(cf. Rand, Binswanger, and Peikoff, *Introduction to Objectivist Epistemology*, pp. 71–74) in question.

# E

**Effect** • An *effect* is the change caused to the configuration of the properties of an entity (e.g., the heating of water changes its temperature).

**Empiricism** • *Empiricism* states that the source of all knowledge lies in sense data (empirical evidence). In empiricism, deduc-tion from knowledge which is not based on sense data is not possible.

**Entity** • An *entity* is a "thing." Something that possesses an identity with properties (e.g., a plant produces oxygen, a stone has a hard surface, etc.).

# F

**Fallacy of the stolen concept** • The *fallacy of the stolen concept* refers to the fact that in the refutation of a statement, the statement itself cannot (implicitly or explicitly) be a part of the refutation. We cannot argue against our existence because the act of arguing presupposes that very existence.[1]

**Free will** • *Free will* refers to the faculty to be able to reflect on our cognition, i.e., to be not determined by external influences. The more one knows about and is aware of what influences him, the more free his will.

# G

*Grenzerfahrung* • *Grenzerfahrung* is German and literally means "boundary expe-rience," an experience that tests our abilities and ideas to the limit.

# H

**Hierarchy tree (of concepts)** • A *hierarchy tree of concepts* refers to the direc-tional ordering of concepts according to their inheritance.

# I

**Identity** • An *identity* is the sum total of all properties of an entity (e.g., weight: 160 pounds, length: 6 feet, has a consciousness, etc.).

**Image** • An *image* is an entity that is linked to another entity by a mental connection.

**Induction** • With *induction*, we con-clude from the special case (a number of concrete perceptions) the general case (the concept). With this, we create new or refine existing concepts, on the basis of sense data and the logical integration of a number of perceptions of entities. For example, if we see a

---

[1] cf. Rand, Binswanger, and Peikoff, *Introduction to Objectivist Epistemology*, pp. 59-60.

number of cars with different colors, we create from this observation the more general concept "car" by using induction.

**Inheritance (of a concept)** • A concept with an *inheritance of another concept* builds upon the other concept's definition. If the concept "table" inherits from the concept "matter," the former would build upon the property "mass" of the latter.

**Integration** • *Integration* is the classification of perceived entities into one or several concepts, as well as classification of existing concepts into more general concepts or a concept hierarchy (e.g., the classification of a perceived sound wave as a definite word, or classification of the concept "human" into the more general concept "life-form").

# K

**Knowledge** • *Knowledge* constitutes sense data, logically integrated perceptions, concepts, or concept hierarchies. It can also be created from logically integrated conclusions from existing knowledge.

# L

**Language** • A *language* is a system by means of which we can translate knowledge of a situation (and concepts) into a series of images and supporting linguistic constructs, and conversely, translate a series of images and linguistic auxiliary constructs into knowledge of a situation (and concepts).

Language is the application of concepts and the hierarchy of these concepts.

**Letter** • A *letter* is a small symbol or image ("a," "b," "c," etc.).

**Logic** • *Logic* is the method of non-contradictory integration of knowledge or perceptions.

# N

**Noun** • A *noun* is a word that stands as a representative of an entity (proper noun, e.g., "Peter") or a concept (common noun, e.g., "dog").

# O

**Object** • An *object* is a noun to which the verb refers as a target (e.g., "Peter throws the *ball*.").

# P

**Perception** • *Perception* is the whole process of sense perception combined with cognition.

**Phoneme** • A *phoneme* is a sound syllable that represents a single unit of sound that a person can make. In the English language, there are about 44 phonemes.

**Pointer** • A *pointer* can be a word, picture, gesture, etc. that "points" to one or more entities. It can be used in their place, e.g., if you "point" to a specific apple by saying "this apple," you do not have to actually take the apple in your hand to make it clear about which apple you are speaking.

**Process** • A *process* describes the mechanism of a cause working to an effect (e.g., if you put an ice cube into a glass of water, the cooling of the water is the process).

**Property** • A *property* refers to the manner in which an entity (or a process) affects other entities (or other processes) in a certain situation (e.g., mass, position, length, name, velocity, etc.).

# Q

**Qualia** • The individual instances of conscious experience of sense data are called *qualia*.

# R

**Rationalism** • *Rationalism* is the attempt to create knowledge without induction and to deduce from this knowledge.

# S

**Sapir-Whorf hypothesis (strong version)** • The *strong version* of the *Sapir-Whorf hypothesis* states that our language determines our thinking; different languages make certain trains of thought possible or impossible in the first place. There is no general translatability of languages.

**Sapir-Whorf hypothesis (weak version)** • The *weak version* of the *Sapir-Whorf hypothesis* states that our language influences our thoughts, making it easier or harder to think or express certain ideas; different languages influence thoughts in different ways, so different languages contribute to different styles of thinking.

**Self-evident statement** • A *self-evident statement* is a statement whose reasoning is contained within itself (e.g., the establishment of the axiom of existence necessitates the very same existence).

**Self-reference (recursion)** • If a statement or a process *references itself*, it is called *recursion*. Examples would be "Read the sentence you are now reading again" (recursive statement), two opposing mirrors in which the images mirror until infinity (recursive process), cell division where a new cell is created that divides itself as well (likewise a recursive process), etc.

**Sense data** • *Sense data* is information, converted to a form usable by cognition, about an effect registered by a sensory organ.

**Sense organ** • A *sense organ* is an entity (e.g., an eye, a nose, an ear, etc.) that is connected to another entity with cognition, and that can register effects of different intensities of properties.

**Sentence** • A *sentence* consists of a number of ordered words.

**Set** • A *set* is a pointer to a number of entities who share properties defined by the set (e.g., the set of the "Seven Seas" refer to the seven oceanic bodies of water of Earth, i.e., the four oceans and the three large Mediterranean seas). Put another way, sets are a way of organizing or grouping entities; they make life easier.

**Situation** • A *situation* consists of a certain number of entities, their changes in properties, their mutual interactions, and their relationships to one another, at certain times and in certain places.

**Structure** • A *structure* is a description of required properties, dependencies, and arrangement of a number of entities (e.g., cube-shaped).

**Subject** • A *subject* is the noun to which the verb refers as an origin (e.g., "*Peter* runs").

**Syntax** • In languages with *syntax*, words can be combined into sentences that each correspond to a meaning.

**Synthetic statement** • A *synthetic statement* is a statement whose assertion is given *not* by the definition of the subject alone; i.e., measurements are required to determine whether it is true or not (e.g., "*This* form has three corners").

**System** • A *system* is an aggregate with a definite structure (e.g., an ice cube, the axioms, etc.).

# T

***Tabula rasa*** • *Tabula rasa* refers to the view that we are born without any innate knowledge and that our minds can create knowledge only with the help of sense data.

**Term** • A *term* is the name of a concept (e.g., as a word or fixed word combination, such as "goods and services" or "in a jiffy"). Every concept has a term pointing to it, but not every term is a concept (e.g., conjunctions like "and").

**Theory of mind** • The *theory of mind* refers to the cognitive skill that makes it possible to understand that another individual may have beliefs and desires that are different from one's own.

# V

**Verb** • A *verb* is a word that refers to the changes in properties of a noun (e.g., an action: "Peter *runs*").

# W

**Word** • A *word* consists of a number of ordered letters.

# Quotation Sources

**xvii:** Beagle, *The Last Unicorn*, p. 1
**1:** Epicurus, *The Art of Happiness*, p. 155
**3:** cf. Rand, *Atlas Shrugged*, pp. 1170–71
**4:** Beagle, *The Last Unicorn*, p. 64
**7:** Wiesel, *The Concept of Heroes*
**9:** Beagle, *The Last Unicorn*, p. 209
**9:** Beagle, *The Last Unicorn*, p. 8
**12:** cf. Rand, *For the New Intellectual*, p. 133
**15:** Ueland, *If You Want to Write: A Book about Art, Independence and Spirit*, pp. 23–24
**19:** cf. Savater, *The Questions of Life*, p. xi
**21:** cf. Rand, *The Return of the Primitive: The Anti-Industrial Revolution*, p. 36
**20:** Keynes, *The General Theory of Employment, Interest and Money*, p. 258
**26:** Rand, *Atlas Shrugged*, p. 969
**27:** Rand, Binswanger, and Peikoff, *Introduction to Objectivist Epistemology*, pp. 59-60
**36:** Peikoff, *Understanding Objectivism*, p. 170
**38:** Rand, *Philosophy: Who Needs It*, p. 90
**45:** cf. Rand, Binswanger, and Peikoff, *Introduction to Objectivist Epistemology*, p. 78
**47:** Sagan, *The Demon-Haunted World: Science as a Candle in the Dark*, p. 171
**49:** Munroe, *Xkcd*
**51:** cf. Knoblock and Riegel, *The Annals of Lü Buwei*, p. 400
**57:** Ueland, *If You Want to Write: A Book about Art, Independence and Spirit*, p. 65
**67:** Turing, *Computing Machinery and Intelligence*
**74:** Peikoff, *Understanding Objectivism*, p. 167
**83:** Feynman and Robbins, *The Pleasure of Finding Things Out*, p. 23
**86:** Feynman, *Character of Physical Law*, pp. 53–54
**89:** Feynman and Leighton, *What Do You Care What Other People Think? Further Adventures of a Curious Character*, p. 14
**102:** cf. Neumeier and Tippett, *Starship Troopers 2: Hero of the Federation*
**105:** cf. Michael et al., *The Grammar of Happiness*
**109:** Hockett, *Chinese versus English: An exploration of the Whorfian theses*, p. 122
**118:** Feynman, *Character of Physical Law*, p. 58
**129:** Quine, *On What There Is*
**136:** Feynman, *New Textbooks for the New Mathematics*, p. 14
**142:** cf. Rand, Binswanger, and Peikoff, *Introduction to Objectivist Epistemology*, p. 69
**169:** cf. Mithen, *The Singing Neanderthals—the Origins of Music, Language, Mind, and Body*, pp. 137–38
**171:** Lawrence, *Memory and Imagination*
**173:** Beagle, *The Last Unicorn*, p. 180
**177:** Ueland, *If You Want to Write: A Book about Art, Independence and Spirit*, p. 8
**179:** Cameron and Wisher, *Terminator 2: Judgment Day*, cf.
**181:** Armstrong, *Twelve Steps to a Compassionate Life*, pp. 199–200
**187:** Feynman and Hoyle, *Take the world from another point of view*

# Bibliography

Armstrong, Karen. *Twelve Steps to a Compassionate Life*. Anchor, 2011. ISBN: 978-0307742889.

Beagle, Peter S. *The Last Unicorn*. Roc Trade, 1991. ISBN: 978-04-5145-052-3.

Boroditsky, Lera, Lauren A. Schmidt, and Webb Phillips. *Sex, Syntax, and Semantics*. In: *Language in Mind: Advances in the Study of Language and Thought*. Ed. by Dedre Gentner and Susan Goldin-Meadow. Cambridge, MA: MIT Press, 2003, pp. 61–79.

Bower, Bruce. *Stone Age Engravings Found on Ostrich Shells*. [online; last accessed June 18, 2013]. 2010. URL: wired.com/wiredscience/2010/03/stone-age-engravings-found-on-ostrich-shells/.

Calvin, William H. and George A. Ojemann. *Einsicht ins Gehirn: Wie Denken und Sprache entstehen*. Deutscher Taschenbuch Verlag GmbH & Co. KG, München, 1995. ISBN: 34-2333-060-0.

Cameron, James and William Jr. Wisher. *Terminator 2: Judgment Day*. USA, 1991.

Cheney, Dorothy L. and Robert M. Seyfarth. *How Monkeys See the World: Inside the Mind of Another Species*. The University of Chicago Press, 1992. ISBN: 978-0226102467.

Dalrymple, Theodore. *Life at the Bottom: The worldview that makes the underclass*. Ivan R. Dee, 1332 North Halsted Street Chicago 60622 U.S.A., 2001. ISBN: 15-6663-505-5.

Deutscher, Guy. *Does Your Language Shape How You Think?* [online; last accessed June 18, 2013]. 2010. URL: nytimes.com/2010/08/29/magazine/29language-t.html.

Epicurus. *The Art of Happiness*. Penguin Classics, 2012. ISBN: 978-01-4310-721-7.

Everett, Daniel L. *Das glücklichste Volk—Sieben Jahre bei den Pirahã-Indianern am Amazonas*. Pantheon Verlag, 2012. ISBN: 978-35-7055-167-7.

— *Recursion and Human Thought: Why the Piraha Don't Have Numbers*. [online; last accessed June 9, 2012]. 2012. URL: edge.org/3rd_culture/everett07/everett07_index.html.

Feynman, Richard P. *Character of Physical Law*. Penguin, 2012. ISBN: 978-01-4017-505-9.

— *New Textbooks for the New Mathematics*. In: *j-ENG-SCI-CALTECH* 28.6 (1965), pp. 9–15. ISSN: 0013-7812. URL: http://resolver.caltech.edu/CaltechES:28.6.feynman.

Feynman, Richard P. and Sir Fred Hoyle. *Take the world from another point of view*. In: 37.4 (Feb. 1974), pp. 11–13. ISSN: 0013-7812. URL: http://calteches.library.caltech.edu/archive/00000035/02/PointofView.pdf.

Feynman, Richard P. and Ralph Leighton. *What Do You Care What Other People Think? Further Adventures of a Curious Character*. W W Norton, 2008. ISBN: 978-03-9332-092-3.

Feynman, Richard P. and Jeffrey Robbins. *The Pleasure of Finding Things Out*. Basic Books, 2005. ISBN: 978-04-6502-395-0.

Hockett, C. F. *Chinese versus English: An exploration of the Whorfian theses*. In: *St. Petersburg Polytechnical University Journal: Language in culture* (1954), pp. 106–23.

Holden, Constance. *How Language Shapes Math*. [online; last accessed May 27, 2015]. 2004. URL: http://news.sciencemag.org/brain-behavior/2004/08/how-language-shapes-math.

Holst, Sanford. *Phoenician Secrets—Exploring the Ancient Mediterranean*. Santorini Books, 2011. ISBN: 978-09-8332-790-5.

Human Knowledge, Institute for the study of. *The Human Journey*. [online; last accessed 3. März 2012]. 2012. URL: humanjourney.us.

Kant, Immanuel. *Critique of Pure Reason*. Penguin Classics, 2008. ISBN: 978-0140447477.

Kant, Immanuel and Gary Hatfield. *Prolegomena to Any Future Metaphysics: That Will Be Able to Come Forward as Science*. Cambridge University Press, 2004. ISBN: 978-0521535359.

Keynes, John Maynard. *The General Theory of Employment, Interest and Money*. Bnpublishing, 2013. ISBN: 978-14-9485-474-4.

Knoblock, John and Jeffrey Riegel. *The Annals of Lü Buwei*. Stanford University Press, 2001. ISBN: 978-0804733540.

Lawrence, Michael R. *Memory and Imagination*. USA, 1991.

Lode, Clemens. *Philosophy for Heroes: Act*. Clemens Lode Verlag e.K., tba. ISBN: 978-39-4558-623-5.

— *Philosophy for Heroes: Continuum*. Clemens Lode Verlag e.K., tba. ISBN: 978-39-4558-622-8.

— *Philosophy for Heroes: Epos*. Clemens Lode Verlag e.K., tba. ISBN: 978-39-4558-624-2.

— *Philosophy for Heroes: Knowledge*. Clemens Lode Verlag e.K., 2016. ISBN: 978-39-4558-621-1.

Michael, O'Neill et al. *The Grammar of Happiness*. Australia, 2012.

Mithen, Steven. *The Singing Neanderthals—the Origins of Music, Language, Mind, and Body*. Harvard University Press, 2007. ISBN: 06-7402-559-8.

Munroe, R. *Xkcd*. v. 0. Breadpig, 2010. ISBN: 9780615314464.

Neumeier, Edward and Phil Tippett. *Starship Troopers 2: Hero of the Federation*. USA, 2004.

Peikoff, Leonard. *Objectivism: The Philosophy of Ayn Rand*. Dutton, New York U.S.A., 1991. ISBN: 05-2593-380-8.

— *Understanding Objectivism*. NAL Trade, 2012. ISBN: 978-04-5123-629-6.

Quine, W. V. *On What There Is*. In: *From a Logical Point of View*. Ed. by Tim Crane and Katalin Farkas. Harvard University Press, 1961, pp. 21–38.

Rand, Ayn. *Atlas Shrugged*. 35th anniversary ed. Dutton, 1992. ISBN: 05-2594-892-9.

— *Capitalism: The Unknown Ideal*. Signet, 1986. ISBN: 978-04-5114-795-0.

— *For the New Intellectual*. Signet, 1963. ISBN: 978-04-5116-308-0.

— *Philosophy: Who Needs It*. Signet, 1984. ISBN: 978-04-5113-893-4.

— *The Return of the Primitive: The Anti-Industrial Revolution*. Expanded edition. Plume, 1999. ISBN: 978-04-5201-184-7.

— *The Virtue of Selfishness*. Signet, 1964. ISBN: 978-04-5116-393-6.

Rand, Ayn, Harry Binswanger, and Leonard Peikoff. *Introduction to Objectivist Epistemology*. Expanded 2nd ed. New American Library, New York, N.Y., 1990. ISBN: 04-5201-030-6.

Reed, Adam. *Object-oriented programming and Objectivist epistemology: Parallels and implications*. In: *The Journal of Ayn Rand Studies Vol. 4, No. 2* (2003), pp. 251–284.

Ryabov, Vyacheslav A. *The study of acoustic signals and the supposed spoken language of the dolphins*. In: *St. Petersburg Polytechnical University Journal: Physics and Mathematics* (2016). ISSN: 2405-7223.

Sagan, Carl. *The Demon-Haunted World: Science as a Candle in the Dark*. Ballantine Books, 1997. ISBN: 978-03-4540-946-1.

Savater, Fernando. *The Questions of Life*. Polity Press, 2002. ISBN: 07-4562-628-9.

Scribner, S. *Modes of thinking and ways of speaking*. In: *Thinking: Readings in cognitive science* (1977), pp. 483 –500.

Texier, Pierre-Jean et al. *A Howiesons Poort tradition of engraving ostrich eggshell containers dated to 60,000 years ago at Diepkloof Rock Shelter, South Africa*. In: *Proceedings of the National Academy of Sciences* (2010). DOI: 10.1073/pnas.0913047107.

Travers, Jeffrey et al. *An Experimental Study of the Small World Problem*. In: *Sociometry* 32 (1969), pp. 425–443.

Turing, Alan M. *Computing Machinery and Intelligence*. In: *Mind* LIX (1950), pp. 433–460.

Ueland, Brenda. *If You Want to Write: A Book about Art, Independence and Spirit*. Important Books, 2012. ISBN: 978-80-8783-058-1.

White, Thomas I. *In Defense of Dolphins: The New Moral Frontier*. Blackwell Publishing, 2007. ISBN: 978-14-0515-779-7.

Wiesel, Elie. *The Concept of Heroes*. [online; last accessed March 16, 2015]. 2014. URL: http://myhero.com/hero.asp?hero=Wiesel_Concept_bk06.

Zimmer, Dieter E. *So kommt der Mensch zur Sprache*. Heyne TB, 2008. ISBN: 34-5360-065-7.

# Index

Is what you're looking for not here? Send us a quick message and help us to improve the index: index1@lode.de

*I believe in you. You can do the thing.*